Dealing With Idiots
Everyday Inspiration For Putting Up With People

Karl Wiebe

DEDICATION

Dedicated to everyone who has successfully
used the self-checkout machine at the grocery store.
Enjoy that bag of grapes—you earned it.

INTRODUCTION

"They" always say that you should write about what you know. "They" say that you have stories inside of you, and you should write those stories! Well, I don't know who "they" are, but they are right. The downside, however, is that the vast majority of time spent on this planet is dealing with dummies. Dummies in traffic, dummies at the corner store—dummies in all walks of life. Dummies don't divide us, they unite us.

Did you know that seventy-five per cent of all people consider themselves above average? Did you also know that sixty-two per cent of all people believe made-up statistics? Whatever the number, I am sure that you consider yourself above average. I know I sure as hell do. Average? Pul-leeeze. Average is the term coined by losers so they don't look so dumb. However, if we drill down on the math even more, we discover that "average" means the half-way point between the best and worst. Uh-oh. It sounds like at least some of us are going to fall dangerously close to average!

I admit it: in some areas of the world, I am a big dummy. If you put me on an airplane and flew me to Switzerland, and then put me in a taxi and drove me to the Large Hadron Collider, and then took me on a tour of the facility so that I could see up close one of the most technically-complicated facilities ever built, would I feel like a dummy? Well, I don't really know very much about colliding atoms and particle physics, so in that sense, yes. Big dummy. But on the other hand, you did just give me a free airplane ride, a taxi ride, and I also billed your credit card for a mini sub sandwich and a vodka Coke during the flight. So now who's the dummy? I'm in Switzerland; I am going skiing. See you later!

Some of the essays in this book are well-thought-out, brilliantly-written prose discussing humankind's struggle against the modern-day technological world—a world where we have grown further apart spiritually and emotionally, despite many of the modern-day communication devices at our disposal.

But mostly it is just me complaining about people that get on my nerves.

Seriously though, I hope that you find these disjointed, completely unrelated essays entertaining and enlightening. Maybe even inspirational? One of my best friends told me that my writing was "great bathroom reading". I'll take it.

Just make sure to flush the damn toilet when you are done.

Karl Wiebe

DISCLAIMER

You might be wondering about the title of this book. "Hey," you are wondering, "am I one of the idiots that this piece of work is talking about? Does he think I am an idiot?"

Yikes. We haven't even started the book yet and already you are yelling and pointing your finger at me I have to respect that. First of all, I admit, not every essay in this book is, strictly speaking, about idiots. In addition to complaining about people, I also complain about machines, television, computers, and other stuff. I also reveal the way the world works. (Well, pieces of the world anyway. The world is a very big place, according to the map of the all-time greatest board game *Risk*).

Need to know why football is the greatest? I will tell you. What is the deal with the *Baby on Board* sign on the back of the car? We might not get all the answers, but we'll have fun finding out.

Okay. Regarding the idiots: I don't know if you are an idiot or not. However, I have a little story that will illustrate who we are talking about.

In Canada, recently they outlawed the penny. Okay, "outlawed" is a strong word—they are doing away with the penny. In Canada we don't outlaw things. We just discourage it and hope that it will go away. In Texas, there is a long and proud history of electrocuting people, gassing people and sticking needles in convicted felons (and they don't wake up). In Canada, convicted murderers are out on the street in less then thirty years. Often they go to jail for less than ten years! We aren't big on the whole "outlawing" thing. So the penny? We asked it nicely to leave.

So this means now that if you are buying something in Canada and the price is $1.54 for example, it just gets rounded up or down.

So $1.51 and $1.52 are rounded down to $1.50.

On the other hand, $1.53 and $1.54 are rounded up to $1.55.

Makes sense, right? It's not rocket science.

Enter the idiot.

I was at the 7-Eleven recently, purchasing my huge vat of Slurpee which I enjoy on a daily basis (don't tell my dentist) and I was standing patiently in line. The guy in front of me is always buying cigarettes and lottery tickets. Every day it is a different person, but it's always "cigarettes and scratch tickets" guy. So this particular guy's total came to $14.96. He had a twenty dollar bill.

I hate to spring a bunch of math on you, so I will help out. You round down. The total payable is $14.95. So... from a twenty-dollar bill, the change works out to five dollars and five cents. Easy.

The clerk handed the guy... five dollars and five cents. Thank you. Goodbye.

There was no goodbye. The guy was adamant that he was owed more money. "You round down!" He started shouting at the clerk. The clerk stood there and nodded. Yes, yes you do. Five dollars and five cents. Goodbye. Goodbye? Please? Even just bye? No.

Now keep in mind: the clerk was correct. The guy got the correct change.

This guy had a meltdown. He was twitching, agitated and started loudly declaring that this clerk didn't know how to do math. At this point, I was reaching into my wallet to pay him two or three pennies— whatever it was going to take—to get him the hell out of the 7-Eleven so that we could all please, for the love of god, move on with our lives.

He finally stormed out. I paid for my Slurpee and was out the door about twenty seconds later. I saw the same guy come out of another shop in the strip mall—the adjacent liquor store—with a case of beer. Was he berating the beer guy too? I will never know. He hopped into his buddy's truck and they squealed the tires and blew out to the street.

Up until now, this guy was out of line, he was wrong, he was a jerk. But was he an idiot?

The truck suddenly stopped. The passenger-side door opened up, and a plastic plate was thrown out onto the curb.

Then the truck squealed up the street, out of view.

Now *that* is an idiot.

So if you are yelling at clerks and throwing plastic plates out of a moving truck, then I am definitely talking about you. And by the way, we all hate you! (Well, maybe not the guy who was driving the truck— after all, he gets some of the beer.) But then again, I seriously doubt that if you are plate-tosser guy you are sitting by the fireplace reading this piece of literature. But if you are, please note that you round down when the price ends with a six. And you are a dink. Don't yell at people and don't litter.

Dealing With Idiots

Karl Wiebe

Why NFL Football is the Greatest Game of All Time

Sports fans are rabid. They love the beer, the TV, other fans (unless they are cheering for the other team) and most importantly... the game. Ah, the game. It doesn't matter—whatever game that may be, it is great. Ice hockey, basketball, football—I've even seen curling fans get pretty riled up. Yes, curling. Picture a 45-year-old woman with a Tim Horton's coffee in one hand, draped in Sweden's national flag, sitting in the stands at the Nokia Curling Brier shouting "Hard! HAARD!" Hey, everybody loves something. I imagine in some bar somewhere in the northern hemisphere, a dart just landed in the triple-twenty and someone bursted into tears, fists in the air.

With me its NFL Football. I love it. Every September, when the regular season begins, my friends and family all say goodbye and I descend into my cave on Sundays. The phone cord comes out of the wall. No one answers the door. Suddenly what happens on a green field in Oakland or Kansas City is of monumental importance to me. But why?

You probably think that you know why football is so popular. After all, it's violent and colourful, loud and exciting. So I'm not going to talk about those things. Everyone knows about the bone-crushing excitement of the game, and therefore I'm not even going to mention the obvious reasons that fans enjoy professional sports. No, what you are going to get is a "behind the scenes", no-holds-barred looks at the real reasons that true sports fans like—no, love—NFL Football.

1) There are lots of breaks during the game. In fact, there's a break after each and every play. It's a long break, too. Unlike soccer that just keeps going on and on, there are lots of times in football where the players on the field are just standing around, adjusting their equipment and scratching themselves. Have you ever watched a football game with some friends? No one shuts up. Everyone talks, and they all talk at the same time. In sports bars, they rarely even turn the sound on, because they know that the

1

people will only talk louder. "What's that? They've turned up the volume? SO ANYWAY, I STILL SAY THAT BRETT FAVRE..." The game has lots of breaks and this lets people analyze the game as it is happening. The television will show each play three or four times. Reverse angles. Slow-motion. Reverse AND slow motion. Super-slow-motion. Stop motion. There's no actual motion on the field, so let's relive that last three-second play again and again. It's great. You can have the attention span of a three-month old puppy and you still see every play during the game.

2) Once every four plays the offense runs the ball up the middle for a total gain of one yard. We've all seen it. You know what I'm talking about. Right after a 30-yard one-handed catch, or an amazing run by some guy with tree-trunk thighs, everyone catches their breath, and then the offense always runs the ball right up the middle. This play always results in a one yard gain. There's a big mass of bodies lying around on the ground. It is the most boring play in football with the exception of the twelve-year old kid who runs out after the kickoff and retrieves the plastic orange kicking tee. No one gets excited about the one-yard run play. "Why do they run that?" The casual observer will ask, just entering the room. "The player only got one yard."

Immediately the hard-core fans will turn their noses up in disgust, as if smelly socks or poopy baby diapers were suddenly dangling in front of their sweaty faces. "They need to establish the run game," one of the fans will blurt out. "The running plays slowly wears down the defense."

Why do the hard-core fans even bother to defend this boring, tedious play? Usually the perplexed novice will leave the room scratching their head. Scoffs of disdain and head-shaking are followed by divorce, although there might be other factors involved. Okay, here's the real deal. The hard-core fans secretly love the one-yard play. This is the opportunity to run to the bathroom, sneak off to the fridge, or pick up that nacho chip that fell on the floor and then eat it when we think that no one is looking. Sure it has a little hair on it, but so what. A chip is a chip.

No one is organized enough to sit through a three-and-a-half-hour game without a pee. This is a cold, hard fact of reality. It's just basic biology. So we love the one-yard run. We aren't missing anything. The big pile-up on the field often coincides with massive toilet flushes around the country.

The only guy who loves the one-yard run for the actual play that it is is one of your buddies who probably played offensive guard throughout high school. Keep in mind, this is the guy who never actually touched the football—he just butted heads with some other big piece of meat across from him for three or four seasons while trying to pass biology class. He has hams for hands and hasn't seen his neck since he was fourteen. He loves the one-yard run.

"Look at the blocking!" He'll yell, eyeballs blazing. You can't hear him, as you are grunting on the toilet in the next room. (You can pee faster sitting down, because you don't need to grab three yards to toilet paper to clean up puddles when you whiz standing up.)

You might call out through the closed door, "what's that? I'm peeing."

"Look at the right tackle block! See the way his foot was over here (waving hands), instead of two inches to the right, over here? (more hand waving)" Whiz. Grunt. Whiz. Flush. Did we miss anything? Not a chance.

3) Every hard-core fan thinks they were "this close" to actually playing professionally. Look at the people in the bar or at the house party watching the football game. Who are these people? Are they big hunky men? Or are they like me? Are they skinny little weaklings who can run really fast? (If so, they are like me.) Why can I run so fast? Hard work? Exercise? Genetics?

No. None of the above. When I played football in high school, I could run really fast. The reason for this is fear. I learned to run fast in high school so the big mean kids with ham hands wouldn't catch me and beat me up. I refuse to feel shame over this. I am fast and proud.

Could I have played in the NFL? A part of me truly believes that if I had only worked harder—if I had only put in the long hours in the weight room, and studied my playbook, or made that spectacular play at the combine and impressed the coaches—

maybe, just maybe, I could have carved out a career in the National Football League.

That part of me is crazy, by the way. No way. Not a chance. I know that logically, the only way I would have gotten a chance to even experience one play in the NFL would have been due to getting bitten by a radioactive spider. (That would be pretty cool). Unless you are really, really fast—like freakishly, world-class fast—or really, really strong, the chances of making a life as a professional athlete are horrible. Remember those high school football guys in your school? The really cool ones who would kick my binder down the hall? Well, only about one in a thousand of those guys ever gets a football scholarship to go on to play university football. That's not the NFL—that's university.

And out of all those university football players that you see on Saturday TV? Maybe one in four or five hundred ever make it to the NFL. You have a better chance of getting hit by lightning AND winning the lottery. In fact, your chances are like, let's say you win the lottery, and then on your way to cash the ticket, you get hit by lightning. No, no even better: You win the lottery, and the cheque is in the mail, and then when you cash the ticket, as that EXACT moment, lightning strikes you, and then you see the envelope with the cheque in it catch on fire (because you were struck by lightning) and then your eyeballs fall out and you actually watch yourself trying to put out the fire. Gross!

The Express Checkout Lane

I will admit it right up front. That's what this book is about—the truth, dammit.

Confession: I count the items before I go in to the express checkout lane. And you should to.

"What's the big deal?" The guy with sixteen burritos is asking, as he reads this paragraph. (Please note that most people like the burrito guy read books while sitting on the toilet. Enjoy your sixteen burritos buddy.)

I'll tell you what the big deal is. We have rules in society. You can't just drive through a red light. You can't just mow your lawn in the middle of the night wearing only shoes. (Trust me on this one.) Anyway, there are rules in place that govern this society. Are we just a bunch of cavemen dancing around a fire pit? Or do we have rules? Who's with me!

But regarding the checkout lane: who at the supermarket made up the rule about the express checkout lane? Was there some "Declaration of Independence" signing of the supermarket constitution where it was determined that twelve items was the correct number of items?

Four score and seven years ago our fathers brought forth on this continent a new supermarket, conceived in liberty, and dedicated to the proposition that all men must not waste everyone's time if all you are buying is a container of margarine, some toothpaste and one bag of nacho chips.

But hold on, someone might be crying from behind their incredibly large and annoying shopping cart. Who said that we can discriminate in our society against those people who happen to have huge families, or shop once every two months, or maybe just enjoy eating tons and tons of food? Who said we could? Me. And people like me. So there.

I don't eat much. I would consider myself normal. When I go to the supermarket, I have twelve items. That's what the sign says: twelve items. It doesn't say "about twelve" or "maybe under fourteen" or "whatever you can carry". It says "twelve items or

5

less". Twelve is the maximum in this particular situation!

So why does the guy with fifteen items feel like he is entitled to just saunter up to the express cashier and pretend not to notice that he has more than the allotted acceptable amount? How does this happen? I once thought that maybe the person in question couldn't count. (I figured this was a long shot, but it was at least technically possible.)

Here's what I mean: occasionally you hear about that one guy who made it up the corporate ladder, and he's an executive vice-president of something-important and lives in a huge mansion with 2.5 children and drives a Mercedes Pompous GL600Z with extra zoom from Italy installed and suddenly it comes to light that all these years, the super-high-executive guy was illiterate!

"What?" All of society says in unison. "How can this be? The guy was an executive Vice-President of the most important thing in the entire company!" But alas it is true. It always seems that there is a story like this about once every couple of years, and it is always just one guy. One guy every couple of years. Do you think they have meetings? All the illiterate executives get together and discuss it?

Chairman: Okay, order, order! Alright fellas. It's been two years. Time is up. So someone has to come clean to the public. Rules are rules! It is either going to be Murray or Harvey this year... one of you has to go public with this whole "illiteracy" thing.

Harvey: I don't want to!

Murray: Me neither!

Chairman: Sorry gentlemen, Harvey said 'no' first. We may not be able to read, and we do in face have these clandestine meetings in airport bathrooms in the middle of the night, but we do have some standards. Murray, you go public.

Murray: I humbly accept the decision of the chairman. I will go and alert the press. Where's the exit? What does that sign say? Exit?

Anyway, my point is that there are people in the world who can't read and yet they live in mansions and have money and children and cars. They know how to function in society. They haven't starved to death, and if they have children, they have had sex at least once. So I figure there must be highly-successful people in the world who are also super rich and powerful, but for some reason they can't count up to thirteen. I know, I know... it sounds implausible. I'm way ahead of you—I originally dismissed this idea as well. My rationale was that anyone who couldn't count would eventually wind up too poor to actually buy food. Every cashier would say something like, "Good afternoon sir, you are buying that small slurpee? And you can't count? That's okay, just hand over cash until I say stop."

Of course, the cashier is not going to say anything to thirteen-or-more-items guy. They have zero incentive to do so. For starters, they are being paid somewhere between 30 cents and 8 dollars an hour to stand there and watch idiots purchase cheeze snacks and then spend five minutes looking for coupons and eventually pay with sweaty paper bills that were stuck in their shorts. Plus, the manager of the store will do literally anything to sell groceries, since that is the only goal of the manager. The manager of the grocery store is surrounded by produce, all of it slowly rotting and wilting and decaying around him. I'm surprised there aren't more managers walking briskly around the store yelling at random customers, "hurry up! Buy these bananas! They're going brown! Please, miss, I'm begging you, buy the carrots..."

My favourite is the guy who is buying forty items and claims that a bunch of some food counts as "one" item. He starts rambling: "these were on sale, five for two dollars!" He will whine, frantically searching for the inevitable coupon. Too bad! Although I wasn't there in your particular supermarket, I can guarantee you that there is no terrorist in aisle fourteen with a gun to the consumer's head ordering him to pick up five bags of bacon puffs. Sure, you can buy five... but go to the other checkout lane. I would like to actually leave the store and feel sunlight on my face before I die from old age please.

Now before you think I am completely heartless, I will confess that there are in fact legitimate foodstuffs that count as one item. Bananas are a great example—if they are all connected, and they all fit on the scale, then that is one item. Grapes are another great example. You are buying one bag of grapes, not 400 individual grapes. Well, let's be honest—402 grapes, since we all know that you put two in your mouth while you thought no one was looking. Am I the only person left in the world who does not feel the overwhelming desire to steal food? Hello, I'm not shopping in Ethiopia. I can wait the fifteen minutes to get home before stuffing my face with grapes. By the way, if I was the manager, I would automatically charge everyone who buys grapes an extra dime because they snuck something into their mouth while they were wandering around the store. Yes, I see what goes on.

Ultimately, we are stuck with the people who will stick a couple of extra items in their cart before hopping into the "express" lane. I guess all we can do is the honorable thing. No, I'm not talking about being more tolerant and realizing that not everyone is considerate. Screw that! I think we should distract them and then steal two or three super-valuable items right out of their cart while they are not looking. We need everyone to work together on this one. Are you a lady with some cleavage? Start bending over to pick up the magazines on the lower shelves. When that happens, I'll grab whatever looks important: healthy foods, vitamins, Preparation H, their prescription medication, whatever. Stealing their toilet paper would be the ultimate, but a missing ten-pound bag of white paper might be noticed. In any event, it will be small comfort knowing that these people get home and are missing whatever they came to the grocery store for, be it delicious grapes, bananas or insulin.

Why Soccer Will Never Win Over North America

It's been called "the beautiful game", but most people in North America grimace with their North-American faces as the World Cup of Soccer invades their television time once every four years. Sorry, Coronation Street and day-time talk shows: your shows are being pre-empted. World Cup Soccer is now on at ungodly hours of the day and night, featuring teams and players that the majority of the world have never heard of.

"Why the big fuss over soccer?" many people ask, befuddled as to why it is so popular. "The big snooze" is how one of my friends describes soccer, or futbol as many "hard core" fans like to call it. (Really hardcore fans will spell it with an umlaut over the u, like fütbol, but I think that is just because they really like the rock band Mötley Crüe or screwing with people's brains.

I personally enjoy watching soccer—sometimes. I'm not a hardcore fan. It's a fluid game, and the skill level is really high at the World Cup level. It's fun to watch a bunch of Africans play soccer against a bunch of Romanians, or English people, or whatever people from the Ivory Coast would be called. Sure, I guess they would be African too, but they wouldn't march around calling themselves African. They would be coasters! Or Ivory people. Well, maybe not. Before I write something that will someday be used in a Human Rights Tribunal, how about we just move on.

My point is: it is fun to watch different countries kick each other in the shins and roll around on the grass, screaming like they are being dropped into a wood chipper.

And that, my friends, brings me to a big reason that many North Americans don't like soccer: the diving. Here we are, watching the beautiful soccer match between African country and European country, and suddenly Tito Von Kukoe (not his real name) bumps into another player, and three seconds he is seen on the pitch, holding his ankle and gasping in pain. A coroner stands by on the sidelines, knowing that no one individual human can withstand so much pain.

9

The referee checks the player for a bullet hole. Was there a second shooter on the grassy knoll? Or was the cleat-on-cleat trip that sent "Tito" to the turf sufficient to put him into a coma? Back up the hearse, the game will break for three minutes while we fire up the crematorium...

But wait! Tito has spied his teammates over on the sidelines, sipping water and doing some light stretching. They have gotten a quick breather and suddenly, like some Southern Baptist ministry, Tito leaps to his feet and is OK! He's been healed! It's a miracle! Let the game continue!

The other big reason that soccer is not much fun for the average North American slob (like me) is that the score is almost 1-0 (one-nil) at the end of a 90-minute match. BO-RING! North Americans are used to watching basketball, where a "defensive" game is still about 120-98. There's a basket every minute! Not to mention tons of breaks, slam dunks, the occasional fisticuffs, commercials, announcers announcing non-stop, cheerleaders, fuzzy mascots and trampolines, and loud rock n' roll and dance music music. Thumpa-thumpa-thumpa gorilla dunk!

Soccer has none of these. The crowd will cheer wildly once every ten minutes or so when there is a shot. Notice I didn't even say a shot on net. Just a shot. Often the soccer player will dicker around with the ball, pass the ball twenty times back and forth, finally get into decent position about a million yards away from the net, and then finally shoot it... but it goes forty feet wide. The crowd still cheers wildly. "Yay! He kicked the ball!" The goaltender is running a marathon every game to try to find the ball.

I enjoy watching soccer, but I don't think we will be cheering the U.S. or Canada with the same passion in a World Cup the way that the Ivory Coasters, English people or people from Africa do. We'll stick to our basketball, mascots and loud rock n' roll music for now. Let me know if the total score ever gets above two.

Sometimes People Just Don't Flush

I don't want you to be reading this whole book and wondering when I am going to talk about people going to the bathroom. So let's get it out of the way right now. Now, there are some people who are going to yell "eww!" and immediately move on to the next little chapter. That's totally cool. But you can't buy only a piece of the book so the joke's ultimately on you. For the rest of us, let me explain why I don't understand the whole "not flushing" phenomenon that has gripped our society.

First of all, let's be clear: not all bathrooms are created equal, and with all due respect to George Washington, not all patrons are created equal either. I was in London last year and I was fortunate enough to attend a rock concert at Wembley stadium. The place wasn't a complete sellout, but there were well over 50,000 people there. I was wandering around outside the massive stadium before the show began, and paused for a second about thirty feet away from the temporary toilets that were set up in a corner, out of the way of the merchandise stands. A gentleman came up beside me and paused.

"Are you in the queue?" he asked in a delightful British accent.

"What?" I asked, confused. I was no where near the port-o-potties.

"I don't want to jump in front of you if you are in the queue," he said. I was thinking about taking a pee and this guy didn't want to be rude! He didn't want to even appear like he was jumping in line in front of me. I immediately felt like hugging this British person. (I didn't.) I was ready to move to England at this point— any country with this kind of manners is all right with me!

Later that evening, I ran off to the washroom (or toilets as it is known in many parts of the world) and there was a big lineup. I thought this was odd—why was the lineup moving so slowly? When I finally got into the bathroom, I was flabbergasted to discover that literally everyone who whizzed went over to the sink and washed their hands. Every single person. That's why the lineup was so slow—people weren't pigs! In Canada and the

United States, you might get thirty-to-forty percent of the dudes washing their hands. (I have no data on the women's washroom hand-washing because I am not a pervert.)

Anyway, hand-washing is the least of my concerns. I don't understand why we walk into a washroom and see someone else's work. Unless your last name is Picasso, flush the toilet! Let me explain.

Colombia is often regarded as the kidnapping capital of the world. When oil workers go to Colombia to work on the rigs, sometimes scary locals jump out of the bushes and kidnap these foreigners. There was a group in Edmonton, Canada who were kidnapped and spent about three months in the jungle while their captors tried to get a multi-million-dollar reward.

Now, I'm not saying that I condone this sort of behaviour. I don't. However, I can at least wrap my head around it.

There's a famous quote concerning crime where a reporter apparently asked famous bank robber Willie Sutton, "why do you rob banks?"

He replied, "because that's where the money is." (Although this quote is widely attributed to Sutton, he denies having said it. I say own the damn quote—it's a good one—better to be known for being witty than shooting people and robbing banks as far as I'm concerned. If you are going to deny a quote, pick something groan-worthy like "Happy Monday" or "TGIF!". The jury is still out on "Happy Hump Day" which is heard around the world every Wednesday. I'm torn because to me, it sounds dirty. To each their own.)

Anyway, back to the kidnapping. The Colombians emerged from the jungle and took some Canadian oil workers hostage, and ultimately the bad guys got paid! The oil company wound up paying something huge like two million dollars to get them back. Now, kidnapping is wrong, but I can think of two million reasons why I might think about doing it. At least it makes sense on a logical level—the Colombians kidnapped the oil workers because that was where the money was.

Using that logic, I humbly ask the court: where is the money when it comes to not flushing the toilet? Let me set up a scenario where I could understand it. Buddy walks into the public bathroom. Maybe he has eaten an obscene amount of squid. I don't know. I am not a medical practitioner, but let's just say that he leaves a souvenir in stall number three. He has the power to flush the toilet, but he chooses not to.

Next up: he climbs atop the public urinals and lifts a piece of the drop-down ceiling tile. He shimmies right up into the grates above the ceiling and peeks through the ceiling grate. He waits ten, maybe fifteen minutes. Maybe an hour. This guy is dedicated. Finally, another dude walks into the public restroom and opens the stall door. Good Lord! The unsuspecting, innocent passerby just bought tickets to Sea World, because something is swimming around the bowl.

Now, if you are psychopath, this is incredibly funny. Buddy is hiding up in the ceiling rafters, silent tears streaming down his face as he tries to hold in his giggling. For you and me, who represent the normal members of society, this seems like a lot of work to get a laugh. I say to each their own. I am not here to judge—if the criminal was still in the ceiling rafters. But he's not. He's long gone. And that's the part that really bugs me: there is no one there to witness the horror on the face of the next person going into the bathroom. Why bother leaving a pile of wet leaves in your front yard if you aren't going to be there to watch people drive by and gasp in amazement? It just doesn't make any sense.

One argument I have heard from people (yes, I have discussed this with coworkers and friends at cocktail parties over the years) is the whole "toilet is no longer working" theory. Come on. I get that in some cases, the toilet is going to be broken. I get it. But that has to be maybe two per cent of the total poop crime docket I would think. So what's up with the other ninety-eight per cent?

Civil engineers have thought about this problem, and they have invented the "automatic flush" toilet now. They marketed it as a toilet that we average boobs don't even have to worry about—as long as we have the ability to either stand up or fall off the side of the toilet, it will flush! That's great, but it bugs me that these bathrooms are all "non-touch" now. There is the automatic toilet, the soap comes out of the dispenser automatically, and the water squirts out if you can somehow manage to get your hands in the exact position to trigger the two-millimetre sensor hidden somewhere under the faucet.

I can live with this progress, but the one that really bugs me is

13

the automatic hand dryer. First of all, we all know that these things never actually get the hands dry. We are all rubbing our wet, disgusting, drippy hands on our shirts or pants just so we can get the hell out of the bathroom before our friends send the police in after us. I prefer paper towels. I like a good dry. I admit it—I like using a healthy amount of paper towel. I double-clunk the machine. I get double the amount that is normally recommended by the paper jury who decided that six inches of paper was the legal maximum that was required to effectively dry hands.

With the paper towel dispenser, now that is automatic as well. It's motion activated. So now I'm doing jumping jacks and kung fu moves trying to get a second helping of paper towel. I'm more sweaty leaving the bathroom than when I came in.

By the way, just so everyone is on the same page—there is a little button on the metal part of the toilet (even the ones with the sensors) that you can push to flush the toilet. You can press it more than once! We all need to work together to make society a better place, and it starts with where we drop our ends.

Computers - Who Needs Them?

You know that there is a conspiracy when the workforce needs a whole group of people who are specially trained to use computers. I'm not talking about "Joe Average" office schmoe who grinds it out for forty hours a week, typing away on their keyboard and doing up the big memo for the middle-level managers. No, the specifically-trained people I am referring to are the "IT" people who spend their days telling office slobs like me to reboot their computers.

Yes, I said conspiracy. You read this correctly. I know what you are thinking. "Gee, isn't that a bit harsh?" Absolutely not and I'll tell you why. And by the way, I'll ask the questions around here!

IT people didn't exist before computers. Do you remember seeing nerdy guys wandering around the office in the 1960s telling people how to use a rotary phone? No way! Pick it up and dial. If you couldn't use the green ten-pound phone with the big "clickity clickity" wheel, then they didn't hire you. That was your IT. You're fired, get out. Learn how to use a phone and maybe we'll hire you back. (The job interview: the company will phone you at home and you have to see if you can figure out how to answer it.)

When the desktop computer was invented, it was supposed to improve the quality of our lives. Has it really done that? For the IT people it certainly has. I am convinced that the IT guys in my office are making money. Why else would they continue to show up for work every day? They have to be getting paid—I'm sure of it. I saw one of them once eating a sandwich. Did he steal it? Unlikely. Not only are they getting paid, I'm guessing they are probably getting that money from the very company that they work for. There has to be something in it for them.

People are idiots, and always have been. There's always one or two (or ten) morons in the office who can't use a computer. Even when they are shown how to hit the "print" button, they still can't grasp the concept and wind up asking again and again how to print something. Hit the print button! It's the same button as last time.

It's always the print button. Tell you what—start hitting buttons. Keep hitting buttons until a piece of paper poops out of the printer.

Before computers, there was probably someone in the office who had to help the idiots with other complicated items such as the stapler, a file cabinet and the office roll of toilet paper.

Example of "pre-computer" IT guys at work:

Office slob: Knock. Knock. Hi, I have a helpdesk request?

IT guy: Oh you must be one of "those people", since you insist on interrupting me in person instead of filling out the help request form in triplicate. I'll just put aside all of these other forms that were filled out correctly and give you all of my attention.

Office slob: Great! I have a question. I was in the bathroom, and took a really huge dump. I ate a lot of chicken wings the night before, and I guess there was a little too much cayenne pepper. Anyway, I wasn't sure how to use the roll of white paper that was in the stall. Can you help me?

IT guy: I am seriously starting to regret shaking your hand at the start of this conversation.

And... scene.

Actually, computers have helped us out as a society, that is for sure. For example, before computers, we used to feel inferior about the car we drove. It's not a Ford GT 2900 model with turbo-charged whatever, so I will never get laid. Or how about the razor? I use one with only seven blades in it, is that enough? No. You loser. Now there's the Mach 4000 with thirteen individual carbon stainless-steel blades. If you shave incorrectly, you will gut yourself like a fish or simply decapitate yourself.

Enter computers. Now, instead of feeling inferior about the car I drive or the razor that I use, I feel "hard drive envy" because everyone else on the planet is using a faster, bigger and more powerful computer than me. Every two weeks these people are running to the Future Zone or Techno-Shack to upgrade their computer. How many gigs you got? You have enough gigs? What about a terabyte? Exabyte? Brontobyte? These are real words. It's depressing. I am waiting for the Infinibyte followed by the You'veGottaBeKiddingMebyte.

I've heard many people bragging about their computer like people brag about their cars. It's like a nerdier version of the hot-rod convention seen on long summer nights out front of the local donut shop. Instead of bragging about their 1976 T-bird with red rims and a rebuilt tranny, they stand around and compare notes about how sweet their technology inside their computer is.

Big bicep dude: Yep, my 1965 Chevy Hot rod. is a classic. Completely rebuilt chasse, all original interior and remodelled johnson rods. She's a hot lookin' machine!

Computer nerd: I know what you mean. My XP 4.9 MHZ petabyte ziggawatt transistor has amazing graphics and a huge 28-inch flat screen monitor. She keeps me company on those lonely nights when my junior high friends and I are not playing Dungeons & Dragons.

Big bicep dude: Similar to all other rebuilt muscle cars, the only down side to my sweet ride is that she still won't actually drive forward. When I turn the key, there's just a gargling noise and she farts out some blueish fluid. When she's not sitting in front of the Tim Horton's on Saturday night, I tow her back to my cinder blocks and get under that sweet, sweet hood.

Computer nerd: How scary it is that we seem to be woven from the same tapestry of life. 'Wanda's' highlights include an additional rigged 18-inch LCD flatscreen monitor that doesn't actually show the colour blue. I can't connect to the internet or actually run any programs at this point. I spent the last three Saturday nights reinstalling Windows XP and Linux to see if I could actually print my name on a piece of paper. Alas, I won't be able to attend the Star Trek convention later this weekend with 'Team Alpha' if I cannot bring 'Wanda' to life. Hu'tegh!

Hu'tegh, by the way, is Klingon for "damn". As if you didn't know that!

I think that the all-time worst thing that was invented in the computer world is the "help" menu. Does anyone ever use these things? First of all, I always hit "F1" by accident when I am actually typing, and then I have to wait five minutes while the "help" menu boots up. Oh, wait, everyone stop working for the next little while, the help menu might show up soon! Some office workers aren't sleeping at their desks—they died of old age waiting for the help menu to load up.

The stuff in the help menus are either ridiculously easy or things that I would never ask for help on. For example, do you need help "changing the colour scheme" in your computer? No! Who cares about the colors? I want to get my work done. I want to print a piece actual text on actual paper, or maybe in my wildest dreams, format the page correctly. How many office workers are spending their days changing their color scheme? Get a life people! I could understand maybe if someone was color-blind and in order to get the big project done he needed the buttons in black and white.

Boss: Why is the project late?

Peon: Johnson doesn't know which button to push.

Boss: Well... did you help him?

Peon: I think so. I told him to hit the blue button, but he just started crying.

Boss: Well, we just lost the big sale. Thanks a lot Johnson!

Peon: Oooh, that is so Johnson.

If only Johnson had changed his color scheme. Thank goodness for IT and computers.

Sick Days

Okay, so I am going to sound like an old man for just a moment. Remember the good old days? I'm talking about the really good, really old days—stuff like World War II. People were considered heroes when they killed Nazi soldiers or parachuted into a POW camp and liberated soldiers. Machine gun fire is raining hellfire upon them, and they just bite harder into their cigar and kept marching up the beach.

More recently, the occasional person gets to meet the President because they rescued a kid from a deep well, or maybe they saved a planeload of people by landing it in the Hudson River. These are heroes.

We are living in a changin' times, my friends. Now the heroes are the people who show up to work even though they are horribly, horribly ill.

"No, I'll just tough it out," they croak, bright green mucus leaking from an eye socket. They gently place a coffee mug under the dispenser, hands trembling. "I have too much work to do." They stagger along the hallway, barely conscious, sneezing and coughing their way into their cubicle. "I'm too important to miss this meeting, cough cough." The next eight hours are spent by co-workers trying to get their own jobs done while not touching anything that the "hero" touched, or breathing the same air. Good times!

Message to the hero: GO HOME ALREADY. You are not the owner of the company. You are some dude or lady in the office with fluid pouring into a hanky. Even if you were the owner of the business... is it really worth it? Just from a selfish standpoint, it doesn't make any sense. Let me explain. For example—let's pretend that you are the boss and as such are probably psychotic. You care about no one in the whole world except you and your company—and your big, fat bank account. And maybe your car. The longer you stay at the office, the greater the chance that you are infecting everyone around you with the plague or whatever disease you are breeding in that walking corpse of a body.

Even if you eventually feel better, everyone else in the office is now enjoying your second-generation germs, which probably mutated when they entered some intern's nasal passages. If one of your office dudes gets horribly ill and dies, you have to replace him! That would be very unlucky for you.

The Home Team

I have a friend of mine who's been a Philadelphia Flyers fan for over twenty years. Like lots of teams in professional sports, in any season they are suffering from injuries and not winning as many games this season as fans feel they should be, and I feel bad for him. This guy absolutely loves the Flyers—he thinks the General Manager is a genius and that the Flyers are the greatest sports franchise in the world.

After saying that, I am sure 99% of the people reading this who are sports fans are immediately throwing down this book and shouting "no way! My [insert team name] are the best! He's nuts!" followed by a possible "let's get him!" And the other 1% reacted with a big evil grin, mumbling "finally! Another Flyers fan. This guy gets it. I am not alone in the world!"

It doesn't really matter if you are in the 1% or the 99% majority; we all have our favourite teams and many of us stick with them through thick and thin.

What really bugs me is when you are cheering for a football team or a hockey team and suddenly that team has some success for the first time in a decade. Fans suddenly start crawling out of the hedges and up from under the floorboards, loudly proclaiming "GO team GO! We love [the only player they recognize]. Sheesh. The rest of us hardcore fans hold up our noses in disgust. Where were they during the hard times? The lean years? What? You were out having a life instead of watching this team lose a bunch of games? That actually sounds like a logical way to spend your life—no, wait, I mean that is outrageous! Shame on you!

But really, when we drill down on professional sports, what are we actually fans of? It can't be just the players, since the roster is continually changing season to season. It seems that everyone winds up getting traded or retiring eventually. We love to throw raspberries at opposing teams' players who used to wear the beloved uniform. It's amazing when a former player comes back to the town a couple of seasons later. Fans are booing and jeering. You bum!

But really, what were the players supposed to do when the General Manager announced that they were going to be traded? Retire in disgust? Resort to physical violence, punch a hole in the wall or burst into tears? Refuse to leave? I think we can all agree that the rational response to a business transaction where a professional athlete is traded to another team would be for that athlete to grab a sword and disembowel themselves like a Japanese samurai.

Can you imagine hanging out in the basement of some hockey arena, and the janitor accidentally discovers someone living in the maintenance area? A whisper emanates from the boiler room. "Is the coast clear? I'm going to go forage for some food before sleeping by the mops," says a Hall-of-Fame defenseman. Wow, one-eyed Frank McGee hid in the bowels of the arena for nine years rather than get paid to play hockey! Now that is a civic hero. Not likely. The players have to earn a living and they head on to the next team, hoping to survive for a few more seasons before retiring.

So what are we fans of? Are we fans of the uniform? Not really, since that too has changed over the years. We've all seen fans at the rink or the field wearing old 1980s-style jerseys. That's great—we're going retro! They are usually awful colours, like easter-egg blue and neon green. Again, that's fine. But here's the question: why are these jerseys always three sizes too small? Either they should buy a new jersey or consider doing a sit up. Were the old jerseys always that tight in the 1980s? Could we see Larry Bird's or Wayne Gretzky's nipples back then? I don't think so.

Since the jerseys change, and the players change, maybe then it stands to reason that we are fans of the owners. No, that doesn't really feel right. I am sure that they are great people and very generous, but I can't imagine camping outside of a big office building downtown and chanting, "go rich white guy go!" as some old person wearing a top hat takes the elevator to their office. What if the CFO's pen runs out of ink when he's signing a big payroll cheque? Does he get booed? I sure hope not.

Maybe, just maybe, at the end of the day it turns out that we are all fans of each other. Maybe it is the communal atmosphere at the arena, the field, or the bar watching our players on television.

Maybe that is what we are really fans of. Through the players we are able to experience the thrill of victory without having to do any actual work like riding a stationary bicycle, learning to skate, or getting punched in the nose. Fans also suffer through the agonizing losing streaks that every team has, and this gives us infinite chances to second-guess the coaches, players and management. It's entertainment, although it changes from one year to the next and even from one game to the next.

We are all fans of each other—I will try to remember that the next time the guy in front of me is taking too long in the public washroom during intermission. Yay team, but hurry up already.

The Pregnant Lady

I'm always reluctant to mention any coworkers because one of them might someday read this book and think, "hey, that person he is talking about sounds really familiar." So... I am hoping that they either don't know how to read, or can't scrounge up the money to buy this book. In my defense, I have worked at a number of different offices, golf pro shops and country clubs, donut stores, and even a fast food restaurant (not to brag, but I was the fry guy), so I am talking generally about annoying coworkers over the years.

I think we can all agree that at times, some co-workers can be pretty annoying, but in my books, the pregnant lady pretty much takes the cake. And I don't mean the actual cake, which she usually takes anyway. After all, she is annoying for two!

Have you ever seen the first-time pregnant woman? Everything is a big deal. If she's in the office and bending over to pick up a piece of paper that she dropped, it's like five minutes. Getting a coffee in the morning? Good luck, you might see her in an hour. She can't lift anything over 5 ounces. "I need help with this creamer for my coffee! Can you lift it up and pour it in the cup? I have to use the stapler; can someone help me please? I'm pregnant, for God's sake!"

Contrast this to the woman who is having her third or fourth kid. Or, heaven help us, her sixth or seventh child. I've heard of this happening. Lady, the Bible phoned and said "tone it down".

By the time the fifth kid is on the way, she just doesn't care anymore. She's proud of all the things she can do on her own.

Me: "Are you sure you should be changing that tire on your SUV?"

Lady: "It's no big deal; I've gone through three or four other babies—I'm indestructible."

Me: "Please, let me pick up the tire jack, you shouldn't be crawling under the actual vehicle while motorists speed by."

Lady: "Honey, just be thankful that everything is still where it should be—primarily under this moo-moo."

When the baby is finally due, the mother just rolls up to the hospital, opens the driver-side door and sticks one leg out. "Let's get this done already... *Survivor* is on in thirty minutes!"

Dumb Sports

There are a lot of dumb sports. A lot of them. Some Americans don't like hockey, and we as Canadian always get offended. "What do you mean you don't like hockey! It's the best! Americans suck!" And then all the Canadians cheer loudly. During the Winter Olympics, Canadians walk around like the Crips or the Bloods. "This is our turf!" we yell at tourists who had the misfortune to go skiing during the Olympic hockey games.

Whether you like hockey, or don't like hockey, I think we can all agree on the dumbest sport of all time. It is... ready for it... the running of the bulls. Agreed? Basically, not getting your genitals impaled by a huge horn is considered a "win". And by the way, when we see clips of it on TV, we're all cheering for the bull, so don't pretend to be all high-and-mighty.

I think a close second to the idiotic "running of the bulls" is... chasing the wheel of cheese down the hill? Have you all seen this? Basically it's a bunch of Englishman or Irishmen or Scotsmen or whatever and some idiot rolls a big wheel of cheese down the hill and then local village idiots just start running down this ridiculously steep hill to try and catch the cheese. People are falling, legs are breaking, people are wailing.

I did do a little bit of research for this book—it wasn't just me complaining to my girlfriend about people chasing cheese and then her yelling "just write it down already! I'm trying to watch television!" Good point and here is the background.

Cooper's Hill Cheese-Rolling and Wake takes place in a place called Gloucester in England. It's a real place; I looked it up on the internet. People roll a nine-pound round ball of cheese down a hill. I'm sure the cow who cranked that out is within viewing distance, and they are looking at this thinking "really? You have completely run out of things to do with the cheese? You know, this did take a bit of work. If you aren't going to take this seriously, can you maybe stop milking me for a while and let me hang out in the field please?"

I don't know, maybe the cheese-chasing village idiots is the dumbest sport in the world. At least the bull runners can brag about the bull. "Yeah, I run down this narrow street and a huge bull with huge horns almost poked me in the wee wee." You kind of shrug and and respectfully admit, "yeah, this guys alright." But what about the cheese people? You see some guy walking in on crutches. "What happened, Johnson?" "Oh, I broke my spine chasing a big wheel of gouda." Yeah... not so macho.

My Dead Body

Cremation vs. Burial. Creation vs. Burial. Cremation! Burial! Hands in the air... what do you prefer? People get so worked up talking about last wishes and what to do with the body and don't bury me and don't cremate me and you'd better bury me and I insist on cremation... blah blah blah.

How about not dying? Is that an option? Cremation and burial are so far down the list for me... I don't care. I just want to live, thank you so much.

Gun to my head, I will pick cremation. Now will you please put the gun down? I think that lying in a coffin is kind of weird. I mean, what's up with the pillow? I know it is called "eternal sleep", but we should all hopefully know that no one actually sleeping. Maybe the funeral guy really thinks that these people are just napping and no one has had the courage to call him on it? "You know, Mr. Johnston, we paid a lot of money for this funeral, and you seem to be really proud of the lovely service... but you do know that Aunty Mimi isn't going to wake up, right?"

My attitude is, if I was going to be buried, I want absolutely no frills. I am cheap in life, I am going to be cheap in death. Stuff me naked into a box and close it up. If I was in a coffin with the fluffy satin and the pillows... what if I woke up? "Hey, this is a pretty good deal!" Except that you are trapped in the ground. Why die again in luxury? I don't want to wake up at that point.

Back in medieval times, there were coffins that were buried in the ground, and then there was a bell in the coffin with a long string attached, so that if the person woke up, they could ring the bell. That is a real thing. My attitude is that if you are going to the extreme lengths to attach bells and strings to the coffin, why not just wait a couple more days? What's the hurry? If there is any doubt that I am dead, leave me alone for another few hours, please!

And can you imagine the conversation with the formerly dead guy when the gravedigger pulls the guy back up out of the ground? Talk about "happy / mad" scenario. It would be like when a kid runs away from home, and then the parents finally find him. The mom grabs her son, tears streaming from her face. "I'm so mad at you, but I'm going to hug you first and tell you that I love you!" That would be the formerly dead guy. He crawls out of the casket and hugs the gravedigger. "I'm not mad at you," former dead guy cries, "but I am going to have a stern talking to with that funeral parlor director!"

The Bruise

You ever get one of those pucks in the nuts? The guys know what I'm talking about. Actually, the ladies might know what I'm talking about as well... not really the nuts part, but maybe you have taken a hockey puck in the boobie or something. I don't know— I'm not a doctor.

We as a Canadian society love to play ice hockey... we're not so wild about wearing pads for some reason. I'm not sure why. You drive by a pond, or a local rink, and you see a bunch of little poor kids who can barely afford skates and they have the beaten-up wooden stick with a crack in it... bad tape job... I can totally understand those kids getting the puck in the nuts. They saved up just to get the stick. They aren't springing for the jock strap. But what about me? I am well past thirty-five at this point. I can afford a jock and proper equipment. But you see ten older guys all out on the pond, skating way too fast and playing with a cold rubber puck. No helmet, no padding in sight! Just blue jeans. Who are you trying to impress? There are no chicks out on the pond on a Saturday night when it's minus fifteen degrees. For some reason, these people hate the tennis ball. It has to be a puck! Newsflash: there are no professional scouts hiding in the bushes.

You ever get one of those horrible, deathly-black bruises on your leg? It doesn't have to be from hockey... could be from anything. We've all got them at some point. They are ridiculous to look at, your leg goes all black and blue and veiny... but it doesn't hurt? That's kind of weird. You might not even notice that you have the bruise. You're sitting there on the bed poking at it with your finger... "hey what is this thing? Did I get abducted and mauled by a bear in the middle of the night? It doesn't hurt! This should hurt. What the hell?" You grab a ruler or a pen or something and start poking at it some more.

Guys love the bruise... when it's visible. It has to be lower down on the leg—low enough that you can roll up the pant leg. For obvious reasons, you can't undo your pants and drop your trousers for any reason at work. This is a human resources thing.

But rolling up the pants, this is allowed. Showing off the bruise in the office is quite the thing for guys. There's always one of them at your workplace... too dumb to wear adequate padding, but smart enough to realize that showing off a big black hole on his leg will get him attention from people. "Eww... that's gross!" Yeah, you better believe it!

The worst, however, is when it's the opposite. You have seriously injured yourself in some horrible way. But there's no bruise whatsoever. You're like in the shower and suddenly "ow". You touch it again. "Ow!" You don't even need to go for the ruler or the pen—you don't need to poke it. It just seriously hurts. But there's nothing there. It's.. regular colour! No deathly black at all! Just skin colour. Boring.

You cannot get sympathy for this. It doesn't work. [Pull up pant leg]. "Hey, check that out." "What?" "Well... you can't see it. But it's really, really sore." Lame.

Sports Injuries

I once worked with a guy who plays rec sports like we all do on occasion. This guy's a young guy, a healthy guy. I saw him limping around the office. I'm like "hey bro, what happened? Why the limp?" And without missing a beat he immediately replies, "Oh, I had a Frisbee accident." Let's all look disgusted at the same time.

Come on! You have got to be kidding me. I wasn't upset that he hurt himself, but I was mortified that he didn't respect me enough to even try lying about it. Bar Fight! Saving college co-eds from burning building! You beat up a celebrity? Orgy gone horribly wrong! I don't care what the lie is. Put some effort into it. We are not going to turn into private investigators and corroborate the story. No one from the FBI is going to knock at your door. "Sir, we've done some investigative work and can find no evidence of you being beaten up by a bunch of naked horny women." Just make it better than 'Frisbee accident'.

Slurpee

There were all sorts of things that were wicked cool when I was growing up that we just don't have anymore. The old people always talk about the "golden age" where all the stuff was great, but it's all relative I guess. For me, the golden age where everything was amazing was the 1980s. And of course, the thing I am talking about that was the most cool thing ever... slurpee collector cups. Oh yeah.

I love the slurpee—always have and always will. (Unless I get diabetes, in which case I will "love/hate" it.) On a hot summer day, I find a cola slurpee quite refreshing. When you're eight years old, you can't really drink a rye and Coke or a glass of wine. "Oh, I don't know about you, but I am bagged after chasing the dog and throwing that baseball around in the park. Time for my grade four homework—where's the Jack Daniels?" The slurpee is all we had.

Nowadays, the slurpee cups are Bo-RING. They just say "slurpee" on the side. Come on people! Back when I was a kid, there were monster cups, rock band cups, wrestler cups, and the coolest ever... the superhero-slash-super-villain comic book cup.

You'd get a slurpee, and the flavour was irrelevant because you just mixed whatever they had on tap... Mountain Dew, Pepsi, Pineapple, grape, root beer... it was disgusting. It was every sugary type of beverage all mixed into one. The flavour was best described as renal failure. No one cared! It was the cup itself that was the best. Superman. Aquaman. Batman & Robin. Lex Luthor. Awesome!

Nowadays, any fool can go to a 7-Eleven and work the slurpee machine themselves and attempt to get more in the cup then on the floor. But back when the slurpee was still a new thing, the guy behind the counter used to be the person who filled up the cup. You couldn't do it yourself. It was like buying cigarettes or the porno mags—trained professionals only, thank you very much. I guess they were afraid that we would just stick our faces under the slurpee tap and just turn it on. Glug glug glug. "Hey, grape face, you need to purchase a collector cup with that!"

So at this particular store, back in the good old days, we could order the slurpee, but we couldn't pick the cup. The guy just picked whatever cup was next in the sleeve and that was what you got. Normally, not a big deal. My buddy gets Superman, my friend gets the Flash, Lex Luthor, Green Lantern, all the cool super heroes are on the side of the delicious beverage of choice.

I got mine. The trained professional hands it to me.

It's Ma & Pa Kent.

You know, Clark Kent's parents? These are the people who were dead at the start of the first issue of Action Comics #1. They are literally eighty years old and have no superpowers whatsoever. And they're dead. I think Ma Kent's power was "baking" and Pa Kent's was "heart attack".

So I've got this lame cup. Why would the comic book company even bother with Ma & Pa Kent? How low on the depth chart of super heroes are you going that you start putting Ma & Pa Kent on the slurpee cup? What was going on in that meeting at DC Comics headquarters?

Boss: We need exactly eighty-seven different cups.

Intern: Um, boss, I'm sorry, but we only have eighty-six superheroes.

Boss: Hogwash! Find something for the last cup or you're fired!

Intern: Either I could create another superhero, write and draw a series of comics and work three hundred more hours... or I can throw two senior citizens into the cup pool. It's five o' clock on a Friday. Ma and Pa Kent—welcome to the big time!

Sitting out front of the store, we were all excited about the different cups that we had. My friends were bragging, "I got the Flash!" "I got Green Lantern!" "What did you get Karl?"

"Uh... it's not important."

"No, really, which one did you get?"

Gulp. "Nah... I think what's important here is that we enjoy our slurpee on this fine summer day. Don't look at my cup!"

Senior Citizens

We've all seen this, any of us who has grandparents. If I was there in person, pretend like I am leaning over like it is a secret.

"The senior's discount?" Wink. Wink.

What is this? Who came up with this idea? Grandpas have been working their whole lives. They are receiving mysterious cheques in the mail like pensions, and old-age security and the like. Some grandpas are worth millions of dollars. I know one senior citizen who stopped paying a mortgage back in 1976. He collects a government pension. He never buys anything nice for himself, ever. We go to the Dairy Queen and he leans over the counter and he says in a low voice, "I'm a senior..." Wink. Wink.

"Uh, okay sir. That ice cream cone is still 85 cents."

Some grocery stores have senior citizens day. It's only one day, and on that day you can give old people cheap food. That's great—get them all in there at the same time and let them go crazy. My only suggestion: shut down the self-checkout that day because they will die of old age before they ever scan their bread.

Yet Another Reason To Be Annoyed With Co-Workers

You ever have one of these people at work? The "easily scared" employee? How annoying is this person. The office is quiet... because, well, people are working, and you walk around the corner to get your print job and you 'startle' the co-worker?

"Oh GAWD!" they scream, at the top of their lungs.

And then, of course, you have to apologize. "Oh I am sorry! I didn't mean to startle you!" Why am I apologizing? Because I was trying to pick up an expense report on the printer?

Other co-workers are derisively shaking their heads in their cubicles. "That Karl... he is so scary, what with the walking and the breathing and the photocopying."

What is this all about? Where are we working, a haunted house? Ooooh, I'm going to make a copy in the mail room. Ooooh.

Politicians

People hate politicians, and I know why. So listen up. It's because they promise things that people cannot relate to. "I'll lower your taxes!" Who cares. "I'll make the streets safer!" Yawn. No one cares about roads or safety. I know how to get elected. All you have to do is promise to make daylight savings time during the day. That's right. Hear me out.

Anyone who's ever worked during the weekend when daylight savings time has had this happen to them. Typically it is some poor sap who is stuck working the night shift at the restaurant or the gas station. It's seven in the morning, but no one is around. Their shift is over. "Uh, hello? Where is everyone?"

The employee working the next shift comes into work all disheveled, a look of confusion and apology on their ashen face.

"Sorry, everyone, I'm an hour late because I don't read the newspaper or watch television or listen to the radio or have any digital clocks that automatically reset the time. I didn't know it was daylight savings time! What time is it? When did this happen? Does this happen every year? I am so sorry."

And it's so frustrating because in the spring, you lose an hour of sleep because we always "spring ahead" in the middle of the night. Vote for me... I'll put daylight savings time at 4:00 pm on a Friday. You're working away, 4:00 pm on the Friday rolls around... boom it's suddenly time to go home. Now we are talking. You want to be president or Prime Minister some day? Daylight savings time.

Fabric Softener

I think that Fabric softener has gotten completely out of control. You want your clothes soft? That is not enough anymore. Now it's "Mountain Fresh" Fabric Softener. Mountain Fresh!

Your clothes are already clean. Your t-shirt just came out of the washing machine. The dirt is all gone. Not good enough! I want them "Mountain Fresh!"

I love it—someone went on some big hike up the Rocky Mountains, he trekked all day, he's got the beef jerky and the back pack and the walking stick—he gets to the top... snow covered peaks, beautiful sunset... takes a big, deep breath.

"This smells like a shirt."

Three-Ply

There's an item in the supermarket you may have seen... I bring to your attention the "three-ply" toilet paper. Three-ply? Is this really necessary? Is two-ply not working out? How soft does this toilet paper have to be? How hard are you wiping that you are tearing off layers of skin down there?

How about some bran? Eat some fibre in your diet. Have you thought about drinking some water? When you are effectively using a pillow to wipe your bum, it might be time to consider having some cereal.

Dog People

Do we have any dog people in the house? Can you raise your hand if you are a dog person? Well, that's stupid, because I presume you are home reading this book, or worse, on the toilet reading this book.

I hate dogs. I am sorry, it's true. And immediately the dog people in the audience are outraged. That's because dog people are like the Jehovah's Witnesses of the animal world. It's not enough that they like dogs, everyone on the planet must also like dogs, and especially their dog.

I am sorry, but if a mammal is going to stay in my house, be smelly, stinky and have bugs... it's going to be me. I work for a living, I bought the house, I alone will take a poop behind the television set thank you very much.

That having been said: I was over at a friend's house recently (well, they are a couple, so technically two friends) and they have a dog. He is a Mexican rescue dog. Someone threw the dog in an oil drum or a dumpster or something like that in Mexico, and a lady rescued the dog and then somehow the dog made its doggy way into Canada.

The dog is awesome. I love this dog. He's quiet, he's clean, he doesn't smell, and he just kind of sits there. I realize why I like this dog: basically he is a cat.

Cat people anyone? If we all got together and went by applause, I can guarantee you it would be way less applause than the dog people. If we had to vote, dog people are out at the bar hooting and hollering, and cat people are sitting at home clicking "yes" in an online poll. This is because cat people don't really like other human beings. They don't come out to shows, they don't really put on clothes and leave the house. They just don't do it.

I like cats because they're cool. They don't give a hoot if you like them. In fact I think they actually prefer it if you don't. Just leave me alone, let me sleep naked with my toes outstretched on this ridiculously huge chair. What's that? A sunbeam? Ah. (Big stretch.)

Dogs, on the other hand, are desperate for attention and it's that trait that I find so undesirable. "Love me, pet me, be my friend!" You want me to be your friend? Are you kidding? Have you seen what I offer to people? I just took a dump behind my television set and you still want to be my friend. I seriously question your taste in companions.

Cell Phones

I hate cell phones. My friends are always telling me that I need to get a cell phone. Come on man, you have to get a cell phone! Meeting me at the mall? Where's your cell? I'll call you on your cell! My friends are always trying to get a hold of me. I don't WANT people to get a hold of me. Don't call me. I will never get a cell phone for my peronsal life.

What did people do in the days before the cell phone? I'll tell you what they did—they showed up on time for things, that's what. No one is on time anymore. Everyone is always running fifteen minutes late. Ring ring. Hey, I'm on the way! No ring ring. Just show up on time. Tell you what: whatever time you plan on leaving... back it up by ten minutes. Problem solved.

Have you seen this? You're in the bathroom, and dude is standing next to you at the urinal? Ring Ring. "Hello? Oh, not much. Just standing here with my dick in my hand. He he he". Then he looks over at me. Never mind me. You're busy. Aim that thing.

Fortune Cookies

I love Chinese restaurants... especially the "all you can eat" buffet. The ginger beef, the sweet n' sour... meat... whatever meat that is... it's all good. However, I do have one part of the night out that gets on my nerves... the fortune cookie.

Who writes these things? Some guy is in a big factory in Taiwan somewhere cranking out 400,000 fortune cookies a month. Do they use a super-tiny typewriter? I can imagine the employee writing these fortunes, locked up in a tiny, dimly-lit room clickity-clacking on an old, rusty World-War-Two salvaged typewriter all day long.

"Hey, Yip Kong, you are a psychic!" the boss peeks his head in once in a while. "Why are you working here?"

"Well," he would reply, wiping the sweat from his brow, "some people would use these powers to one day win the lottery, or maybe go on the road and market their incredible psychic abilities as a showman on stage or television. Maybe some people would become super heroes, knowing that certain events were going to transpire, and that they could, somehow, save untold lives from misery, injury or death. However, I've always been attracted to long, repetitive hours of manual labour. I love to type. Now, back to work!" Clickety-Clack.

I wonder if fortune-cookie guy in the warehouse ever spills a skid of cookies. He's driving around the forklift, moving 300-pound boxes of tasty fortune cookies filled with flavour and winning lottery numbers. The boss comes wandering over and sees the huge pile of spilled cookies. "Seriously, psychic guy?" he asks the fortune writer. "You're surprised? You didn't see that coming?"

Water Level

I was taking a drink of water out of the fountain at work the one day. Normally the fountain is crystal clear, ice-cold water. It is very refreshing. I work hard, I occasionally deserve a drink dammit!

The water level from the fountain is always the exact same. It's always right at "mouth level", which works for me because I happen to have a mouth pointed right at the water. However, this one day something strange happened.

I pushed the button, and the big curve of water started up. Just as I was about to take a sip, the water level dropped about three inches. At that exact same moment, I heard the toilet flush in the men's room just a few feet away.

Insert sad trumpet sound here. Wah-wah-wah-waaaaaaaah.

Yes, I know that water all comes from the same place. Yes, I know that there are "filters" to prevent whatever I was thinking.

But... I don't care—I want the water level to remain constant, even when the toilet is flushing. Especially when the toilet is flushing. Bleacch.

PVR

If you are under forty years old, you have heard of the PVR. PVR stands for "personal video recorder" and is also sometimes called a DVR or a "digital video recorder". (Thanks Wikipedia!)

I was a VCR guy for the longest time. I think I outlasted pretty much all of my friends. In the long race against technology, if I didn't win this one, I definitely finished in medal contention. Most of my friends would have arguments (they would call them "discussions") that went something like this:

Helpful Person: Hey are you PVRing the big show tonight?

Me: I will be recording it on my VCR.

Helpful Person: What?

Passerby who heard that I had a VCR: "Ack! My heart! I am dying!"

Me: I am sorry that you are dead. I am taping the show.

See? At least I am polite. Anyway, I had a VCR and a regular television set. Nowadays it would be called "standard definition", but I called it "television". People were literally begging me to buy an HD television, knowing that I would love to watch sports and actually see what is going on.

I finally bit the bullet and after three years of constant research, reading every technology magazine and countless hours of wandering through every store from Wal-Mart to Sonny's High-Tech Devices & Mattress Emporium, I finally bought an HD television set.

The TV is huge. It's 52 inches. That's a nice size if you happen to live in Saddam Hussein's old palace. Unless you are opening up your own movie theatre, you do not need a TV that is that big. But, because I am a guy, I demanded that I "had" to have one of these. What about sports? What about movies? I had completely forgotten that for the past thirty years, I had watched the football game and Police Academy 3 on my rinky-dinky 20-inch TV and that was perfectly fine. But not now! Now when I turn on my television, it is like an LED power ring at a professional hockey game. I'm a guy and those are the rules.

The reason I bring up the TV issue is that with high-definition television, the picture is crystal-clear. The picture is amazing. You can see things that you don't even want to see. If you are ever going on a television show, you had better make sure that you have properly exfoliated before appearing. If it is broadcast in HD, check your teeth too. A piece of broccoli in the little gap in your teeth? Two million people just saw it.

So I bought the HD television, but I still had the VCR. When you tape a show using a VCR, and then play it back again, the HD aspect is gone. The "H" is gone. In fact, the "D" is pretty much gone as well. It is like you are legally blind, but you decided to watch a TV show anyway. You go from high definition to no definition. Absolutely nothing is defined. You are just watching blurs trying to catch a football. Or, more specifically, blurs just trying to catch a blur.

So I finally relented to the crushing, relentless force that is "society" and bought a PVR. "This will change your life," my friends would bark at me, Tony-Robbins style. People who never show any emotions would talk about the PVR and suddenly become Dr. Phil or Richard Simmons. Their mother had passed away four weeks earlier and they never cried, but when I mentioned the PVR, their faces lit up and tears welled in their eyes. "Who's ready to PVR?" My Richard-Simmons like friends would start doing jumping jacks. Okay, okay—I bought it already!

I totally admit, recording a show in HD is pretty cool. With a PVR and an HD television, you can watch a high-quality show. The problem is, unfortunately, that there are very few high-quality shows. Sure, the shows themselves are being broadcast in high definition, I'm just saying that it is the same garbage that has been on television for the past twenty years. Just now it is in HD.

There is some stuff I can totally understand being in HD. For example, movies are great for HD—here you have a cinematic masterpiece where the director has painstakingly laid out a story, with themes layered on top of each other, and the viewer is drawn in to a beautiful and haunting film about life and tragedy. But, enough about Weekend At Bernie's numbers one and two.

Watching a football or a hockey game in HD is pretty neat. I feel like a tabby cat watching a fishbowl or possibly a bird through the living room window. My eyes dart around at the movement and occasionally I let out a little chirping noise.

However, I do question why things like the local news and the weather has to be in HD. Really? There was a shooting at the local cheque-cashing place and we need to see the 19-year-old store manager in HD?

I guess I shouldn't complain—after all, whenever I go outside and open my eyes, the whole world is in HD. I guess the weatherman should be too.

Going Topless

Naturally, any story revolving around a nude beach or nudity of any kind should start in a donut shop. That's just good writing.

Years ago I was working at a donut store, baking donuts in the middle of the night. I started my shift around 11:00 pm. It was a great job—the radio station was playing, the muffin guy was cranking out some carrot cake... it was a well-oiled machine.

The manager of the store was a good guy and would come into work around 7:00 am, just as I was finishing up. One morning he walked briskly into work, coming in through the front door and bypassing the lineup of patrons buying their daily coffee and donut. The boss made his way into the back kitchen area where I was mopping the floor.

"You will never believe what just happened!" he practically screamed.

"Okay," I said. Who was I to argue with my boss?

"Do you remember that lady who was wandering around downtown topless?"

I admitted that I did. About two months earlier, before the snow started flying, some lady decided that she had the right to wander around out in public without a shirt or bra on. It was a human rights issue—perverts everywhere in town knew all about this story. There she was, just waving in the breeze. Apparently the police had a problem with her walking around near the downtown showing off the nipples, so they gave her a time out.

The topless lady sued the city... and won! Cheers went up around town by everyone—women, guys who enjoyed wearing trench coats... it was a story that really brought the city together. So it was determined that it was totally legal for women to walk around topless. Burn your bras ladies! Or just take off your shirts. Either way.

My boss was so excited. "You know what this means?" He said, his voice way too loud considering there were people twenty feet away trying to buy a crueller.

I thought about it for a half-second. "Well, I imagine that it means that eventually we will see scores of half-naked women roaming the streets in packs, like wild animals," I suggested, trying to make him feel better.

"This is the greatest thing ever!" He yelled.

I couldn't take it anymore. I walked over to the little doorway that separated the front of the store from the back kitchen area where I worked.

"Take a look," I suggested.

Confused, he glanced out the door.

"Anyone out there you want to see with their top off?"

His demeanor instantly changed from what could be described as "horny" to "suicidal".

He learned an important lesson that day, one that most good-looking women seem to instinctively know: most people that you see naked in real life, you don't really want to see naked.

Mystery Sick Days

You may remember earlier in this book I was "having a go" at people who think they are heroic by staying at work, even when they are clearly sick with the plague.

There are, however, employees who do the exact opposite: they take sick days for any conceivable reason whatsoever.

I heard a story about one employee who had to take a sick day because they put their contact lenses in a cleaning solution, and then put them in their eyes. Really? You had to take an entire sick day?

Well, that's a great story, but I think I'll turn "Ironside" here and cross-examine the witness. Hmm... you have two eyes, don't you? And you put in your contact lenses one at a time? Don't you think after the first lens burned like a blowtorch in your eye socket that you might have paused before putting the second contact lens in?

Case dismissed. Phony.

Typically when employees have to take a sick day, they send at the very least an email to their boss. For a lot of jobs, though, you have to actually phone the boss. The boss wants to hear your voice. You know that they are secretly judging how you sound on the phone and wondering if you are really sick.

Employees counteract this by doing anything possible to get the voice mail. [Phone rings] "Sorry, boss, I'm sick today. I thought something was up when I had searing, unbelievable pain in my left eye. I thought it might be the contact lens, since it started the instant that I put the contact lens in my eye socket. But, I wanted to make sure, so I went with the other contact lens. Boy, I wish I hadn't done that. So now both of my eyes are in horrible pain and I'm pretty sure it is the contacts. I'm like 90 per cent sure. I don't know why I didn't put my contact lenses in proper solution before bed—I went with the pickle brine. I am starting to really regret it now. I'm going to wait it out for another couple of hours, just to be absolutely certain, and then maybe I'll try washing my eyes with dish soap or small pebbles. It's a good thing I memorized the layout of my house and I have you on speed dial, or else you never would have heard from me!"

Where I live we get quite cold winters, but during the dark, dreary months we might get a week or two of mild weather. This, too, also presents problems. In the middle of January, it could be deathly cold (which is expected) or it could be above freezing (which is a nice treat for a few days). Warm weather apparently affects the joints, muscles and the ever-mysterious "migraine" headache. It warms up, and suddenly the sick employee is suffering a mysterious headache that is based on the weather.

I love the migraine, because no one can verify it. "Ah, my head is killing me!" you groan, looking like you've taken a bullet from the sniper in the watchtower. Okay, sure thing... if you say so. I like to turn on all the lights in the room when talking to the employee, or occasionally blast an aerosol air horn randomly just to see if they are annoyed by that. If they act annoyed, then their story holds up—they must have a migraine.

Of course, if you mention that maybe they should go to the doctor, the employee will invariably cry, "oh no, I just need to sleep it off." Really? You're going with the "hangover" plan of recovery with this one? Instead of waiting in the emergency room at the hospital, or driving to your doctor's office for a last-minute consultation, you just need a bag of potato chips and a flat-screen television at your place to get rid of the mysterious headache. Sure, we get it.

I always wonder why these people with "warm weather" migraines are always the same people who wind up going to places like Mexico and South America for vacation. You realize that these countries have warm weather twelve months of the year, right? Wouldn't the airplane land, the big door open and your head just explode right there on the tarmac? I'm very confused.

When I worked at a golf course years ago, in the pro shop, I saw one employee show up to with a broken foot once. This was apparently a huge deal. He was on crutches and could barely move. My entire day was spent on the lookout for this person. If you happened to turn a corner and they were trying to open a door, suddenly you turned into the doorman. If they are in the nearby kitchen trying to "get food" then suddenly you turn into a five-star chef. "No, no, let me heat up this leftover pizza for you in the microwave!" you have to yell at them, loud enough so that other co-workers won't think you are a complete dink.

Now, I know what you are thinking. "What a heartless guy! How can you be so selfish?" The answer is easy: I have work to do! Quit spending your time trying to re-heat pizza in the microwave. You can't move. Pick up the phone and order in. The delivery guy will put it literally on your desk. Instead of going to the bathroom all the way down the hall, try grabbing an empty wastepaper basket and scream at your co-workers to turn around or all look east at the same time. (If you are going to try this method, use a plastic waste bin—not the metal ones with little holes in them).

I saw this employee waddling down the hallway with their crutches on their way to the water fountain. People would hang their heads and half-smile with sad eyes in an attempt to throw some sympathy to the injured employee. "So brave... even with a cast, still trying to nourish themselves." Of course, the employee in question has now turned into the "false modesty" person, where they spend half of their day deflecting sympathy while at the same time trying to appear as pathetic as possible.

By the way, they still haven't gotten to the fountain yet. They are still waddling along. They were barely moving, with their foot uselessly dangling in a cast. I mean, they were really going slow. Terry Fox ran halfway across Canada; I'm pretty sure I could get to a water fountain thirty feet away with a broken ankle in a reasonable timeframe. You still have a good ankle—didn't you ever learn to hop?

"I'm sorry I couldn't get this spreadsheet completed—I'm really suffering over at my desk with this broken ankle." Really? It's your foot that's broken, right? Have you turned into Koko the monkey, keying data at your desk with your toes? We'll ask the bosses to hang a tire swing over by the fire escape for your fifteen-minute break. I mean, if you sit at a desk and key or type, you literally just need fingers and some eyes. Really, if times are tough, you just need one finger and one eye. That's the minimum. A pirate with a hook for a hand could still key data into the computer no problem.

HR Representative: Wow, did you see Blackbeard over in accounting? That guy has a peg leg and he's keying data like a madman! I waved hello but I don't think he saw me—I was probably from the 'eye patch' side.

Vice-President: I know what you mean. If you give Captain Hook in Human Resources a high-five after he types up the memo, go for his left hand.

Actually, come to think of it, working with the occasional pirate might not be all that bad. Being a guy, I am well aware that the men's washroom in an office or a restaurant is usually rated somewhere between "awful" and "absolutely disgusting" by the end of the work day. At least it would be easier to tell who wasn't flushing. "Um, boss, I think I found out who isn't flushing. I think it might be Redbeard in payroll. I don't want to stereotype, but he does have a peg leg and I could see it under the stall door. Although, to be fair, Johnson in accounting is quite a billiards player, so maybe he's bringing in a pool cue while he's taking a poop."

Bless You

Heaven help you if you are within earshot of anyone—and I mean anyone—who sneezes. If it's a co-worker, the race is on to see who yells out "bless you!" first. If you are at the mall, minding your own business, and a perfect stranger sneezes, then you must shout out "bless you!" or you are labelled a horrible human being by passersby. You know who else didn't yell out bless you? Hitler. (Probably.)

"But, I don't know this person!" you can yell at strangers as you stand next to the person who sneezed. Everyone is making their way from the Wal-Mart checkout to the parking lot, giving you the "head shake". Dude, it doesn't matter if you don't know the person. You have to say bless you. I don't know why, I don't like the rule, but somehow that is what everyone has agreed to.

If someone gets a microscopic particle in their nose, or if they inhale a tiny hair, or if they walk by an open pepper container, or even if they are thinking about onions or stinky feet, get ready to shout out blessings like you are the Pope. (Okay, I am guessing at that last one. But I imagine that stinky feet make at least someone in this world sneeze, and do you really want to take the chance of not being prepared?)

Bless You. In advance. Now leave me alone and let me shop for toiletries at the Dollar Store in peace.

The Doctor's Office

Do you know what the average life expectancy of a human male is? Neither do I. I think it is around eighty years old. A lot of it depends if you are a middle-aged white guy in North America who detests physical labour (like me), or if you are smelting heavy metals in China for two dollars an hour.

In the ancient days—like the days when Greek people wore togas and sat around being all philosophical, the average age was around thirty years. That seems young to me. But then again, we have to remind ourselves that a lot of babies died right out of the gate so that probably brings the average down. But either way, people were not living a long time. That's why we see only a few really old Greek people in the statues (and on the cover of pizza boxes). All hail Little Caesar!

If you are wondering why I am thinking about this stuff, it is because I am trying to kill twenty minutes as I sit naked in the doctor's office waiting for my physical. Because of "flu season", they even took away all the magazines. I don't have a subscription to People magazine; how am I supposed to know "who wore it best"?

I just turned forty, and that means that my days of partying all night with a cocaine mustache and then kicking the strippers out the door and falling asleep in my bathtub are over. They are also over because they never actually begun. How about this: more specifically, my days of eating two Big Macs and a large fries, and a chocolate milkshake, and staying up until 3 am playing a World War II strategy game on the computer are long gone. (I always played as the Soviet Union during my World War II video game nights—that probably explains why I go to the doctor twice a decade; it's part of Stalin's "five year plan".)

I showed up to the doctor's office on a typically snowy winter day and announced that I was here for my physical. I promptly took a seat and noticed that I was literally the only person in the doctor's office. When do you see that? For me, it had been never—usually these clinics, where multiple doctors work, are one step above a Rwandan refugee camp. It's a little cramped is all I'm saying. Maybe everyone else was cured? Is my doctor that good? Then I wondered that maybe my doctor was that bad—no pesky repeat customers. Either way, The Better Business Bureau won't be getting any calls in regards to your practice!

Anyway, after my obligatory fifteen-minute wait, the nurse (I'm going to tell myself that the person with the flip chart was a medical professional) came and got me and we went to some clandestine back room.

The lady who I at this point was hoping was a nurse ordered me to take off my jacket because I was going to get weighed. I suddenly felt like Muhammad Ali. I stripped off my winter coat and ripped off my hoodie, ready to jump on the scale and show the nurse that I was in shape. I knew that I weighed 180 pounds, but then I wondered when the last time was that I went to the bathroom. That skews the results, people. My big plan was that I dropped the hoodie on the chair in hopes of bringing my weight in line with what it should be.

Apparently it's either tough to read a scale, or math is hard. It was one of the two. The big number said "150" and the small number said "29". It was literally two minutes of me standing there while the lady added up the two numbers. "You're 169?" She asked. I didn't move. "No... 159!" She announced. I remained. "Hmmm... 179?" I immediately stepped off of the scale. Yay, you got it right! You won a prize... me! On your dream date, you get to take me to the back room and watch me put my hoodie back on. Then the date is over.

I was thrilled to be in Canada, where these people don't bill the client. This person had shown that numbers weren't her "strong suit". If she was doing the payroll, the staff were either getting paid hundreds of thousands of dollars, or they were going three months without a cheque.

I was internally laughing until I got back to the little room and sat down. She instructed me to strip down to my underwear and wait for the doctor, and then she shut the door.

I don't get this part of the whole operation. I mean, I was wearing a t-shirt, jogging pants, underwear, two socks and a smile. That was it. If there was some sort of emergency, like a radio DJ suddenly showed up to the doctor's office and was handing out a thousand dollars to the first three people to strip naked and run out into the lobby, I am pretty sure I would have been a strong contender. I sat there, fully clothed, and waited. I was taking a stand (sitting down).

This is when the questions about life expectancy started, by the way. If a human male lives to be about eighty years old, that means that I am basically halfway there! That was depressing. Then I pictured myself living to one hundred. That was also depressing. On the one hand, I would probably look and feel terrible. Happy one hundred, can you hear me? No? Okay, time for bed, it's 3:00 pm. Even if I was one hundred years old and super healthy, what would be the point? Most of my friends live marginally healthy lifestyles. They travel, eat red meat and enjoy the occasional drink. Between heart attacks, diabetes, liver failure, and plane crashes, the chances of me having any friends at one hundred was slim to none. I made a promise to myself that I would eat healthier, exercise more, and start befriending little children. I killed that idea immediately because I realized I didn't need to sound any creepier. I figured I would just wait until I was eighty and then start making friends with adults. I would be "cool old guy"! Everyone loves that guy. I'd be like the William Shatner of the group.

I still hadn't taken off my clothes. Where was the doctor anyway? What is going on in those other rooms? If you are that sick, go to the hospital. Otherwise, get in and get out.

Instead of just doing what the nurse-like-lady said, I started thinking of reasons to remain fully clothed. The only one I could come up with that was reasonably logical was that it was winter and I was cold. I wasn't going to take off the shirt. This whole thing was ridiculous. I was getting angrier and angrier. Then I heard shuffling by the door and immediately, instinctively whipped off my shirt. Whiff! I was topless in one second.

It turned out it was just some person walking by the door. I was outraged. What was up with this doctor? Who is doing all that loud walking out in the hall? Why was this taking so long?

I spotted a thermostat on the wall on the far side of the room. When I say "far side", I mean it was about four feet away. The room was a broom closet with tongue depressors. I started seriously weighing the options: what if I stripped down, but also cranked the heat? That would teach them a lesson! I pictured the nurse-ish lady getting the heating bill a month later. "What? Eight hundred dollars to heat this tiny office?" Yes, but remember that naked guy who sat in there for two hours and turned your little waiting room into a Swedish sauna? Well Doctor, maybe next time you will want to show up on time!

The Winter Olympics

Once every four years, average, normal people in North America and Europe lose their minds. They go crazy for the Winter Olympics. Now, as a sports fan, I can kind of understand the "human interest" that the Olympics has to offer. I mean, don't we all want to know who the fastest human being is? And when the guy breaks a world record in running, we can say with a certain amount of awe, "wow, that guy is the fastest person who ever lived!" That is pretty cool. We have a certain fascination with marathon runners—did you know that the first marathon runner comes from the legend of Pheidippides, a Greek messenger who ran from the battlefield of Marathon to Athens without stopping? He burst into the meeting of the Greek assembly to announce that their army had won the battle and then collapsed and died. See? Now I don't feel so bad when I get chest pains going for a walk down the street to the 7-Eleven. It's not natural.

Anyway, my point is that the summer Olympics have roots back to ancient times that feature the Gods, cool stuff like battles and fighting lions and basketball. (My research may not be 100% accurate but you get the general idea).

Fast forward two millennia and about four yawns and you get the Winter Olympics. I don't get it. Sure, everyone in Canada (and a few in the United States) love hockey, but what about the other sports? Biathlon? What is that? Who thought it was going to be a great idea to combine cross-country skiing and then shooting a rifle at a target?

How did this event begin? "Gee, I really want to assassinate my boss, but that snowstorm is really putting a damper on my plans. Well, I guess I could just call him up and apologize for losing that big account... but I am a good skier... and come to think of it, he does have a window office."

I would be really nervous of the fans at an event like this. Imagine for a second that the skiers are all rounding the bend, and the whole crowd cheers! And then the one athlete drops down into the snow, breaks out his sniper scope and his huge, exploding bullets and proceeds to hit the target from fifty yards. Ping! When you hear that noise, immediately look around the stands for that one loner who is rubbing his hands and showing a little too much enthusiasm at this point in the competition. Chances are good that this is the guy who will wind up being interviewed from prison on an upcoming episode of *Dateline*.

Who's Ready To Rock?

We all love going to rock concerts. What's the best part? The incredible, rancid odour of pot? The jet-engine like decibels of every piano key, guitar note and shriek? How about the incredibly expensive ticket prices? You want to sit in the lower bowl? Please talk to our finance agent who will set you up on a twenty-year amortized plan. Enjoy the show!

Seriously though, I do enjoy a good rock n' roll concert. For me, because I am old, bands like AC/DC and KISS put on a great show in my books. For one night I can pretend to be eighteen years old again—my incredible immaturity finds a home for one night—for two hours I am surrounded by other old men, some sporting mullets, but mentally we are all surrounded by high school kids and university students still "searching for that major".

My personal favourite part of the show is when the crowd gets a little tired and quiet—and then the lead singer comes out and asks the crowd some questions:

- Who's ready to rock?
- Who likes to party?
- Who's ready for some alcohol?

All of these questions are designed to elicit a response, usually in the form of "wooooo", a fist pump, or if you are a woman, taking your top off. These are all acceptable responses to these questions. "Let me ask you this... is [your town] the greatest city ever?" and the panties come flying up on stage.

What I don't understand is why the lead singer of any rock band is always deaf. No matter how loudly you cheer the first time, it will never be good enough. Example:

"Who's ready to rock?"

Crowd cheers with wild abandon.

"I can't hear you!"

Crowd now descends into chaos, shrieking like banshees, lighting fireworks, shooting off mortar rounds and running around, wild-eyed, looking for blood. Loud fans surround a small group of security guards, ripping off the arms of one guy making ten dollars an hour and using them as weapons against the other guards.

It's gotten to the point where some of us "old timers" won't even cheer during the original question. "Who's ready to rock?" Silence. Young fans look over at me in horror. "Hey dude, he asked you a question!" I just shrug. I'm not playing that game. When I was twenty, I shrieked like my genitals were on fire and it simply wasn't good enough. It wasn't good enough then, it wasn't good enough now. The rock star repeatedly told me that he could not hear me. I'm not falling for that again.

Of course, the rock star inevitably says that he can't hear us, and we scream even louder. This second time, I join in. Hostile, angry fans who noticed my earlier snub now come around and realize that my cheering was the microscopic addition to the 20,000 people cheering that somehow pushed it into an acceptable range for the billionaire onstage. The rock star nods approvingly and the show continues.

Just once I'd like to see the lead singer query "who's ready to rock?" and when the crowd goes completely mental with cheering, screaming and fist-pumping, he yells into the microphone "Whoa! People! Calm down! It was a simple question... no need to get rowdy!"

Special Parking Spaces

What do these three sentences all have in common?

- "Harry the Unicorn will be heading up the accounting department."
- "Congratulations on that promotion! Your hard work and showing up on time is finally being rewarded."
- "Hey, look at that parking space open right next to the mall doors!"

Answer: none of them have ever happened, to anyone, ever.

Generally speaking, I hate the mall. I try to avoid the mall during the weekend. Or during daylight hours. Or ever. Have you ever wondered who is at the Wal-Mart at 7:01 am on a Saturday? That's me. You see more people at the Emergency Room and in the International Space Station orbiting Earth than you do at the Wal-Mart in the early weekend hours. I guess all the hillbillies like to sleep in. Disclaimer: We tease because we love, and I consider myself a hillbilly so I can make fun of "my people". (I also consider myself a senior citizen, both sexes, and also every conceivable race and orientation for the purposes of making fun of people. We are all human beings dammit.)

Of course, the people who design the malls aren't thinking about parking. That is the last thing on their mind. Forget the parking spaces. They want more shops! More concessions! Spend MORE MORE MORE! And then when the one rational guy on the project asks about parking, the fat cats and big wigs just laugh and tell Skippy the intern that the consumer can take the bus, or possibly ride a clown car with 19 other people so that they can find the last remaining parking spot. Hey, with 20 people in a car, you are saving the environment at the same time! Bim Bim the Panda and Kimshu the Killer Whale thank you.

As you enter the third hour of circling the parking lot, you are now looking for any conceivable opening, whether it is a legitimate parking space or not. You start to look at smaller cars and wonder if you can just do "squeezies" in between them. You start actively cursing and flipping the middle finger to large trucks in general—their drivers are long gone, inside the mall, but you are flipping off the remaining vehicle. "Who do they think they are, taking up an ENTIRE parking spot?"

Stress levels are rising as your fuel gauge is creeping closer to the "E". Why is no one leaving the mall? What is so awesome in there that not one person has decided to call it a day and head out to their car?

Once in a while you will see someone who looks like they are heading to their vehicle, and you trail them like a private investigator stalking a serial killer. The car creeps along, at ten feet an hour, following this senior citizen as they slowly make their way to an automobile. They open the trunk, deposit their shopping bag... and then turn around and head back inside! At this point, you have two choices: rage, or pretending that you weren't really trailing this guy for the last ten minutes as he was walking to his vehicle. This is when I look over at him with an expression like "What? What's the big deal? I always drive the speed of a tortoise in a snowstorm. I like to be safe. It's not always about you!"

Eventually, after a painfully long time, you spot the empty space, but it is within walking distance of the mall so your mind dismisses it. This cannot possibly be true. The spot is located right in the front of the parking lot—it is right next to the mall. You creep over, telling yourself that it can't possibly be. No one ever actually parks in these spots. People who find these coveted spots just leave their cars there, in the spots, all year round. They will take public transit home. You imagine the conversation around the dinner table: the wife asks "honey, where's the Ford Fiesta?" The husband shrugs, that look of complete and utter satisfaction on his face. "I left it in the mall parking lot about three months ago—I can't mentally accept losing that space, so I think we should seriously consider buying another car. We can visit the Fiesta on weekends by taking the number 72 bus down to the Forest Heights Mall."

As you slowly creep up on the space, there is that split-second where you realize that it really is a blank, open space. It's just sitting there.

You start to cry. It is so beautiful.
And then you see it.
The handicapped parking sign.
Of course! It was too good to be true. This is the oasis of parking lots. Now at this point, a number of things are racing through the average person's mind.

First, you consider parking there. Most religious people immediately discard that idea and figure that they are going to hell for just thinking about doing such a thing. Can you imagine if this was true?

At the gates of Heaven

Me: Hey guys, how's it going. I died. So I guess I'm checking in.

God: NOT SO FAST!

Me: I know what you are thinking. Thirty years ago, I saw the spot, I wanted the spot—let me finish—I did NOT park in that spot.

God: IT DOESN'T MATTER! It's a sin to even think about it.

Me: If I had known that I would have actually done it. And a few other things. Actually, come to think of it... a lot of other things. A. Lot.

God: Yeah that really sucks—tell it to the chief of police.

No rational, able-bodied person ever actually parks in the handicapped stall. We all know this. Parking in the handicapped stall is barely one step above having unprotected, dirty relations at a bar with a stranger. I've never personally parked in the stall. I've thought about it. I've fantasized about it. But I've never done it. Yes, we are still talking about parking!

So it is settled—I am not a dink—so I would never park in the handicapped stall. I have, however, seriously thought about jumping out of my moving car and lying down in front of it on the pavement. The automobile would crush my foot and I would be sufficiently "disabled" to warrant parking in the stall. If anyone wanted to give me a hard time, I would show them my mangled foot and immediately make them feel like the big dummy. How do you like my crushed ham for an ankle, you big jerk!

People would walk by as you are judging me and of course I would start sobbing, with the quivering lip and the crushed-ham ankle (a "hamkle" if you will), so most passersby would wonder who the creep is that is making the guy with the flat shoe cry. The hard part would be avoiding the rocks as the general public stones the dude who actually wanted to make me move my car.

And then of course, there is the one action that we have all done, but hardly anyone ever admits to doing: we spy someone else pulling in to the handicapped stall, and they get out... and they look perfectly fine. We see the "blue wheelchair pass" hanging in the car just under the mirror—obviously some government official somewhere deemed this guy disabled enough to warrant parking in the Shangri-La stall located ten centimeters from the mall. We start wondering: kidneys? Fake leg? Some sort of growth under his shirt?

"He had better be pretty disabled," we grumble, doing our tenth lap like we're riding some sort of ride at the evil carnival.

The mall parking lot is the only place on earth where handicapped people are being stopped on their way to their cars and congratulated. "Hey, sorry to bother you—a bunch of us over here were just hanging out and we saw the stall. Nice work. We are so jealous of you!"

I still haven't figured out why a person in a wheelchair needs to park closer to the mall than me. I mean, I have to walk! That guy literally has wheels. Often the wheelchair is motorized. If anything, that guy should be parking further away! He is literally driving to the mall, parking and then driving into the mall. That just doesn't seem fair. As I watch the guy in the wheelchair roll out to his car, I always think "why do bad things always happen to me?"

I know that being jealous of a guy in a wheelchair will probably mean I am going to hell. But I figure I am already going there—five years ago I thought about parking in the stall for a split-second so I figured I might as well run with it.

The Vacation Tan

I am a white person who lives in Canada. This means that when I am on vacation, I must go somewhere sunny and warm. Winter in Canada is pretty much nine months of the year. (The other three months are known affectionately as "construction" or "mosquito" season).

When winter is most of your life, Mexico, Cuba and Hell are all acceptable vacation destinations. The planet Venus would also be acceptable, although the travel time leaves a little to be desired. The minute that any white tourist steps off of the airplane in Mexico, the race is on: how much tanning can this person get in one week?

If you are like most people, and you are staying at an all-inclusive resort in Mexico, everything revolves around the tanning. Everything. Get up before the sun comes up! As soon as there is a tiny red sliver on the horizon, the eyes blip open and it is time to get moving. Go have breakfast outside and wear a short-sleeved shirt. Did you ever wonder who that red, burned guy is eating sausage and eggs while wearing a wife beater? That's probably me. His nose is peeling off, his skin is bright pink, but he has to tan! I look like a honey-glazed ham on the beach.

It's so stupid. Why do we do this? Why do we spend a week at the resort wandering around with minimal clothing, cursing at every cloud and spending every evening looking in the mirror at our pigment? Because, for most of us, we eventually have to go back to work. And it sucks. We will be back with the other pasty white people, and we want tangible, visible proof that we actually went somewhere nice and warm.

"Hey, look at Johnson in accounting! Was he in a four-alarm fire? His nose has fallen off and all of the skin on his ears is gone."

"No, he was in Puerto Vallarta eating shrimp for a week!"

And we can't complain that these people look like Freddy Kruger, because we are pasty and white. All we can do is save our pennies, and when we get down to Mexico, whip off all of our clothing and try to instantly tan.

Travelling For Business

Have you ever been to the mall on a Tuesday afternoon, say around 2:00 pm? The place is packed. Some people work in an office all day, while others always seem to be "out". Rarely, on occasion, I will be allowed out of my work cage early and I get to drive around in traffic in the middle of the day. I always ask the same question: Doesn't anybody work anymore? Am I the last person who works a full-time job during the day? Where are all these people coming from? I am beginning to wonder if I alone am keeping the economy going. All these highways are being paid for by my income tax. You are welcome!

Recently, I was asked to travel out of town for work for a week. I stayed at a pretty nice hotel in the middle of a downtown city in a foreign land. Well, okay, it was a charter bus ride three hours north of my home, and still in the same province, but you get the idea.

The first thing I noticed about my behaviour was that upon my arrival in my hotel room, I immediately looked at everything in my immediate surroundings like a 1970s-era Soviet refugee. Soap, shampoo, toilet paper— all of these things were prized possessions that would be smuggled out of the hotel in my suitcase when I left. However, I figured I could do one better. I was staying for a few nights, not just one—why not round up all of the toiletries in the room and throw them in my suitcase right now? The housekeeping staff must think that hotel dwellers are the cleanest people on earth: "I can't believe it, Johnson in room 293 used up another two litres of shampoo! He must be eating a lot of fiber as well, since the four rolls of double-ply toilet paper are also gone." I'm surprised the hotel doesn't keep their linen on big chains like the pens at the bank. I can't say I would blame them.

Before you start crying in sympathy for the hotel chains, don't. The hotel gets us back in other ways. You want a roll of toilet paper? Okay, you hobo, we are charging you FOUR DOLLARS for a Mars Bar. They don't even have a vending machine; they just put all the M&Ms and candy bars right in a basket in your room and then just tell you that they will bill you if one goes missing! What is that? Now I am suddenly running confectionary security for the hotel? "Sorry guys, I can't go out tonight—someone has to stay here and guard the Skittles and bottled water."

Nude Beaches

When you are a thirteen-year-old boy, at least once a day you think about nude beaches. That is just a fact. But I'm not telling you anything you don't already know. Pretty much any legal nudity is on the minds of any teenage boy.

However, there is one major problem with the nude beach for guys—and no, it isn't "where did I put the keys to the convertible." It all boils down to the fact that guys can't exactly "hide" when they look "interested" in what is "going on" while at the beach. You catch my drift? Actually, catching a cool drift sometimes does that as well. Suddenly, you are asking people to start calling you Mount Suribachi because near your midsection there is an Iwo Jima flag-raising going on. Yes, a little World War II humour mixed in with erections. No refunds.

I wonder if anyone has ever just gone to the nude beach with a pair of binoculars, or even better yet a camera. Just no shame whatsoever. The dude is just wandering around, snapping pictures and then when someone is outraged, the pervert agrees that the camera is "garbage" and they are going to buy a new one just as soon as they "sell some photos to raise some cash". One of my favourite jokes is asking someone if they know who the most popular guy is on the nude beach. The answer: the guy who shows up carrying two ice cream cones and a dozen donuts.

Gift Cards

Imagine life back in the 1960s—Dr. Pepper was like twelve cents, mobile gaming devices consisted of a tire swing or a stick and a tennis ball, and cash was king. This was the time when there were no credit cards—there was a card called Diner's Club, which was one of the very first "general purpose" credit cards, and there was also MasterCard (or MasterCharge, as it was known back then) and Visa. However, these companies and cards were really in their infancy and not many people (certainly not many middle-class people) used these cards on any massive scale. No, if you wanted to send a birthday gift that was valued by your nephew but required minimal effort on your part, you stuck a 5-dollar bill in a card and mailed it. Done deal—I'll think about you next year, little Billy!

Now we have gift cards everywhere. Walk into a major department store or a grocery store, and there is an entire wall filled with gift cards. Wait a minute—the whole store is filled with food and products, and that is not enough. Here's a wall where you can buy stuff that will allow to buy more stuff. Enough already!

The best part about the gift card is that it is just like cash, except less convenient. Wow. How did this ever catch on? "Hey, where do you want to go for lunch?" If you have cash, you can go literally anywhere. But the guy with the gift card suddenly starts narrowing down the choices. "My Subway gift card means that we can go anywhere in the whole world... that serves Subway sandwiches! As long as it is within city limits." Argh. Put that fine dinner in Paris on hold—we are trekking down to the local Subway over by the bus station to eat an assorted sub.

The Filthy, Filthy Barbeque

Right now as I write this, my barbeque is sitting eighteen inches from me. "What!" you may be screaming. "Are you writing out on your deck?" The answer is no, and please don't take this the wrong way, but stop screaming. Actually, I am sitting in my computer room. Yes, my barbeque is sitting in my home office.

Long story short, the condo association decided it would increase the value of the property by replacing the railing out on the deck and replacing the flooring on the balconies. Great! Unfortunately, that means that I have to take all my crap that I normally store out on my deck and throw it in the condo. There is a reason that we keep old lawn chairs, patio umbrellas, and greasy, stinky barbeques outside on the deck. That stuff is gross. So, as I write this essay, I am danger of hitting my head on a metal spatula if I lean too far back.

The only good thing that has come from this is that as I write, I can smell hamburgers. The downside, however, is that I know that the smell is actually three-year-old meat grease that is sitting in a used tomato soup can, hanging from the bottom of the barbeque because of a skillfully-placed, rusty, twisted coat hanger. Yummy!

What is the deal with guys and barbeques? Have you ever seen a guy cooking in the kitchen? Maybe reluctantly it has actually happened. For most of us men, we not only have no idea what we are doing, but we also don't care. Read directions on the side of the frozen pizza box? Bah! When the pizza is brown (or black) then we know it is done. If we are supposed to cook it at 400 degrees for thirty minutes, why not cook it at 4,000 degrees for three minutes? I am in a hurry! Halftime isn't going to last forever, I need to get this stuff done. I am sure that at least one guy working at a nuclear power plant has looked at those radioactive rods and wondered how quickly it could cook a hot dog.

Yes, most guys aren't really into kitchens. However, you get that same dude who is clueless in the kitchen and throw him outside onto a deck or patio, and suddenly he has turned into a master chef. Litres of different barbeque sauces instantly materialize. Honey mustard, Dijon everything—pepper, cilantro, it all comes out of the woodwork. Aprons and Chef hats make an appearance. We get it, we get it—you are awesome, you know how to burn a steak.

I didn't realize how filthy my barbeque was until I brought it into my home. It is really quite horrific. I can't believe that I cook food in that thing. Can you imagine if you treated your oven like that? If I see one piece of soggy macaroni on the stove top, I have the normal reaction that most people do—I freak out and grab the dishcloth. A raisin falls under the stove and I am spending a half hour with a broom and herniating a disc trying to get that morsel of food out of there and into the garbage can.

Remember when you were a kid, watching your mom cleaning out the oven? Most of us remember something, because the smell was similar to mustard gas during World War I. She would be armed with elbow-length rubber globes, some sort of bandana or surgical mask, and spraying the inside of the oven with some horrible biological agent that was powerful enough to get the United Nations to at least think about authorizing a surprise inspection. What were we cooking in there that is sticking to the wall like that? Was mom cremating small animals in there while I was out at school? What a great business idea—is that why we could afford to eat at a nice restaurant twice a year?

Afterwards, the oven was shiny porcelain white or some other beautiful, classy colour. These days, the ovens are often stainless steel but they are still spotless.

Meanwhile, there's a horrible hailstorm outside, beating the barbeque with frozen acid rain pellets and we shrug, because we already have our juicy barbeque hot dogs. Why cover up the barbeque? We're busy and the game is on!

The worst of all is in the spring, after the long winter finally disappears and the air is warm enough to warrant standing outside to cook a burger. We open up the barbeque and there could be any number of horrible things going on in there: spider webs, some mystery stain that may or may not have come from the inside of a bird, or possibly a possum or small racoon living in the grill. If any of these things were to happen to our oven, we would immediately throw it out and buy a new one. Can you imagine if a bird pooped on your stove? The stove is gone. Instantly. What about if a squirrel crawled out of your oven? Goodbye oven. Possibly goodbye house. Meanwhile, we just have one solution and one solution only for any of these problems if it is a barbeque. It doesn't matter what the problem is—just turn up the heat to maximum for about ten minutes. "It'll just burn off," we tell ourselves. Bring the meat, we're ready to cook!

Office Licking

Unfortunately, many offices have a shared printer. This means that decent, hardworking guys like me have to put up with all sorts of weirdness because other people are, well, gross. Whenever I print a piece of paper, I get up from my desk, walk over to the printer, and pick up the piece of paper. When I say "pick up the piece of paper", I mean that I reach out and grab the paper, and then return to my desk. I do all of this because I am not a crazy person.

I have worked in a few different offices and places with printers, and I have determined that I am the only human being left with any sort of moisture coming out of my pores. Everyone else seems to be some sort of human-lizard hybrid, since they need to lick their fingers repeatedly in order to pick up any sort of paper. The worst part is that they feel the need to be "helpful" and lick-grab my paper for me.

Licky the co-worker: Is this your print job?

Me: No.

Licky the co-worker: Are you sure?

Me: Yes.

Licky the co-worker: It has your name on it.

Me: What's that over there?

And then I run away, hoping that Salty Von Lickenstein goes home early or gets distracted by a bird or something.

Overhearing Inappropriate Office Conversations

What's worse than overhearing an inappropriate office conversation? I contend that it is worse to overhear only half of the same conversation.

We all know that at least a couple of people who have jobs are unfortunately disgusting. For some reason, they are hell-bent on sharing all of their health problems. If your life is truly a train wreck, why tell everyone?

You are on your way to the printer, or coming out of a meeting, or on your way to take a whiz, and you overhear two old ladies in the hallway, their voices low (but not low enough). You only hear half of what they are saying, and it usually goes something like this:

"… and that's when I said to my husband, 'either go to the doctor and get that checked out, or go sleep on the couch!'"

"…I just feel like my doctor is making a big deal of it because it is located so close to my genitals."

"….Once it started turning solid again, I figured that it had run its course. I am glad I can eat carrots again!"

"…the handkerchief was destroyed, and we had to throw it out, but I was able to describe what I saw in there to my doctor and he really thinks we have a shot at beating this."

Take my advice and just keep walking! Speed up if possible, even if means possibly running over a fellow co-worker. The first priority is protecting your sanity.

My Guide To The All-Inclusive Resort

By this part of the book, you are no doubt dehydrated from laughing at all the hilarity. But wait! Didn't you also buy this book for advice? So far, it has been non-stop entertainment. Time for this bus to turn the corner and start edu-taining as well.

Before we start learning, let me ask you a question: have you ever been to an all-inclusive resort? Yes? Then it is pretty obvious to everyone in the universe that you are a gluttonous pig. Hey, I happily include myself in that group. Yay for us! Oink oink. These hotels, nay, paradise resorts, sit on the beach in some tropical part of the world where coconuts and bananas just spring forth from the earth the way stinky, wrinkly mushrooms do in the cold Pacific Northwest, or the way dirty snow puddles pop up pretty much everywhere else north of the Mason-Dixon line.

For those poor slobs who have never been to the all-inclusive resort, you may be asking yourself, what's so great about the resort anyway? Let's all take a five-minute time-out while the readers who have been to the resort tilt their heads back and laugh like drunken hyenas. Which, strangely enough, is exactly what most people sound like when they sit around the pool bar hot tub at these very same resorts.

All-inclusives normally exist in places like Mexico, Cuba and Jamaica. Resorts in these countries can offer these inexpensive Roman orgies of food and drink because

a) that is the part of the world where booze comes from and
b) that is the part of the world where really cheap labour comes from

Take Cuba, for example. Being a Canadian, I am legally allowed to travel to Cuba. A bunch of us were sitting around a big, fat table with our big, fat slushy rum punches and our big, fat guts hanging out while our beautifully-tanned, toned waitress came by with another round of big, fat slushy drinks. Vacation is the best.

She pointed over to a middle-aged man who was setting up shop about thirty yards away. We learned that for only thirty dollars, we could enjoy a one hour massage! "That's an incredible deal!" said the overweight pasty-white guy with a six-inch beard. He had spent the last eight months of his life working at a research station in the Antarctic. He told us that he had spent about twenty-two hours a day in his submarine-like bunker of a science facility, with dim lighting and getting his news from his laptop computer. There had been no women at the station. I was a bit nervous that he was going to enjoy this massage too much.

At the end of the day, as the hot Cuban sun slowly sunk down under the beautiful horizon, I staggered over to the massage therapist and introduced myself. I asked him how he became a massage therapist. In communist Cuba, had Fidel Castro ordered him to do this line of work? I pictured the military all lining up and the leader walking briskly past, dictating what each member's role would be. "You! Machine Gun. You! Sniper. You! Rub people's clavicles and glutes."

The massage therapist was quite professional; in fact, I learned that this guy was a medical doctor! Like all Cubans, he worked directly for the government, but he was given two months' holiday per year and he spent half of that time at the resorts picking up extra work. He told me that he got to keep a portion of the money that he made performing massages—he was able to keep about half of the money that he took in, and the other half he turned over to the government.

It didn't sound like a lot of money to me, and then he dropped the bombshell: he made almost as much money in a month of massaging people as he did the entire rest of the year as a doctor! That sort of information I found mind blowing and, quite frankly, stressed me out a little. He was on to my little game and told me no free massages. Fair enough—these Cubans sounded like they were only in it for the money! I had to respect a communist who would only work if he was getting paid—I saluted his work ethic as I squatted back down at the bar and shoveled another frozen margarita into my mouth.

The point is, the labour down in this part of the world is really cheap, and that is why it is important to tip when you are at an all-inclusive resort. Have you ever used those "travel" websites where people can rant and rave about how awful their hotel was? Every time I go to Mexico, Cuba, or anywhere sunny, I scout out the hotel online. I don't know why I do this—every single place I have ever stayed at has been fine, and every single place I have ever looked at online has had terrible reviews. It seems like if you go on holidays, and you have a great time, you come back home and get on with your life—work, home, watching television, buying groceries, et cetera. You never think about the online review after you have had a good vacation.

But if you go to Mexico and you have a crummy time, the only passion that remains in your life upon your return home is to write a novel online about why this placed sucked. The service? Deplorable! The food? Disgusting! There were bugs everywhere! One of the tiles by the pool was loose and my idiot son almost broke his toe! I had to wait in line for five minutes in order to be seated at the restaurant for my sixth meal of the day! This is unacceptable!

These people are never happy, and personally I am glad that they have a terrible time at these resorts. Since you bought this book, and thus you are essentially begging me for advice, I will give you some. Here are some tips on how to enjoy yourself in Latin America:

a) Slow down. You are on vacation. Put away the watch. You don't have to be back at your terrible job for a whole week. So chill out and if that means that you have to stand in line for five minutes in order to get two more free drinks, so be it. Take the time to look at some bikinis. Or smell some flowers. However, do not smell the bikinis—this will not endear yourself to the other tourists. Trust me on this one.

b) Eat healthy and familiar foods. There is so much food at an all-inclusive resort that it is easy to just go hog-wild and try everything. This is a sure way to wind up with your face stuck in the toilet three days later. Things like cooked meat and vegetables are great, because they are cooked. Don't eat a lot of seafood or raw vegetables because sometimes they contain bacteria. Sometimes the dairy in other parts of the world can be a bit different on our systems as well. Cows are not all the same! Drink lots of water because it is usually 4,000 degrees outside and too much booze will make you throw up. (No, I am not a doctor. I know this from experience.)

c) Tip the wait staff. You work hard, right? Right? Well, let's pretend you do for the sake of this argument. When raises are handed out by the boss, would you like one? Of course you would! Now imagine if your boss walked over and said, "instead of a raise, I am giving you something more valuable." You start salivating. Then he puts out his hand. "Shake my hand and accept my thanks." Really? That is more valuable? You would have to buy a new pair of dress shoes because one would be lodged up his ass faster than you can say "disgruntled". That same general idea applies in Mexico, Jamaica, or wherever there are hard-working staff helping you enjoy your stay. Make sure to tip. Thank them to their face, with a smile, and give them a dollar! Here is a little "bonus tip" just for you: when you are going for a meal or drinks, tip at the start of the evening instead of the end. This way, the wait staff already know that you "get it" and will be your best friend throughout the evening. Give it a try! If it doesn't work, make sure to go home and write all about it on the internet. Or you can get a life. Your call.

Visitors In The Workplace

Has this ever happened to you? You are working away at your desk, and suddenly an email shows up:

The Vice President Of Importance is going to be touring your office this week. Kindly remove all debris, make sure your workplace is tidy and free of clutter.

What I want to know is why anyone at the Vice-President level is walking through the trenches where low-level data entry guys like me are working. I become immediately suspicious when I see this sort of behaviour. And why are they so wound up about a few cluttered files in a cubicle, some papers sitting on the office floor or dirty underwear hanging on a bent clothes hanger? It just seems so overly dramatic.

On the day of the arrival, co-workers are going to be running around like headless chickens as a limousine slowly crawls through the parking lot. "He's here, he's HERE!" one of the managers will squeal, turning away from the blinds while trying to not pee their pants. Staff will be deployed to the washrooms to ensure that all the toilets have been flushed. (Temps will be dispatched to the men's washroom to manually pull any chewing gum or paper clips out of the urinals.)

The Vice President will arrive looking immaculate—top hat and tails, cummerbund and tap-dance shoes that are so black that no light escapes from his feet. He will twirl his moustache and look at my workspace through his recently-polished monocle. "Yes... yes..." He will run a white glove along the edge of my desk and then closely inspect the damage. "Yes! This one passes!" I will then breathe a huge sigh of relief but I will be careful not to have any "relief spittle" hit my workplace.

A few minutes later we realize that Johnson over in marketing was let go—although he had stellar performance reviews and never missed a day of work in eight years, a stale corn chip was discovered in-between his recycle container and the wall's electrical outlet.

Security escorts him out and he spends the next six weeks at home, feverishly vacuuming his apartment in-between sending out resumes.

Social Media

If you are over sixty, please put down this book and walk over to the telephone machine and dial up your grandson. Ask them what social media is. As they LOL, or possibly "R" on the "F" laughing, you will understand that the next generation of slackers are all connected via the interwebs. Your generation marched on Washington and fought for civil rights; this generation is tweeting about which Real Housewives of Orange County is their hero.

Actually, it is not that bad. In the 1980s, the internet was born when a group of computer nerds at universities connected their mainframes and formed a loose network of computers that "talked" to each other. They were able to share research and write notes to each other on bulletin boards. This was in the days before graphic-heavy internet was in full use, so most dirty pictures on this new web consisted of a dot-matrix ASCII picture of a penis, like this:

=======()

Yikes! Sorry about that, I should have warned you that there would be graphic content in this essay.

(.) (.) Boobies!

Or maybe that was creepy eyeballs... who knows? The eighties were a crazy rough time.

Nowadays, however, virtually everyone is on Facebook, or MySpace, or Twitter, or whatever new media site pops up. There is only one important feature in order to make this sort of thing successful: it has to allow people to voice their opinions about the most trivial, boring things imaginable.

See, Facebook says that their goal is to allow you to "network with friends". But what makes Facebook really popular is that you can constantly bombard your friends with updates about the trivial minutiae of your life. It is the computer-equivalent of walking around your neighbourhood like a five-year-old beating an old rusty cooking pot with a wooden spatula. Look at me! CRASH! CRASH!

Here are examples of Facebook status updates that represent what marketing guys want us to think about social media:

Karl Wiebe "is organizing a protest of the prison conditions in Burma at 9 pm downtown. Let's show the man that we care about human rights!"

Karl Wiebe "is looking for help for a special date with my girlfriend. Can anyone recommend a great restaurant?"

Karl Wiebe "really likes that his friend Graham Smitticock rode his bike for five days straight to raise money for cancer research. Great job Smitty!"

Wow, it sounds like Karl is really connecting with others and sharing meaningful experiences? Yes, that is what the marketing gurus would like us to believe.

Remember, however, that there is marketing and then there is reality. Here is what really goes on when people update their status:

Karl Wiebe "is going to eat the McIntosh apple. Yes, it is really going to happen this time—sorry about the ten other posts that were false alarms. Once eaten, I will post a five-page synopsis of said apple".

Karl Wiebe "just woke up. Not sure if I should brush my teeth or take a huge 'bathroom break'. I will advise via my iPhone what I decide, probably as I am doing it."

Karl Wiebe "is really happy that the 'thing' happened last night... you know what that means if you are the one person that this pertains to. But I am sure that all 500 of my friends are happy that they spent 30 seconds of their lives reading this cryptic, completely uninformative post."

You have the chance on Facebook to "like" a status update. I wish there was not only a "dislike" button, but a voting button, and then at the end of every month, the person with the most votes would get a knock on the door, and a stranger would kick them in the genitals and confiscate their computer or iPhone for a period of three days. Repeat offenders would lose their phone upwards of a year. However, no matter how many times they won the vote, they would only be kicked in the genitals a maximum of one time. (After all, I don't want anyone out there thinking I am a monster.)

The Royals

I don't "get" royalty. I am not sure why everyone is so fascinated with the Queen, for example. Prince William & Katherine Middleton (the media calls them "Wills & Kate") were married at Westminster Abbey and it was a beautiful ceremony. I was more impressed with Westminster Abbey. Did you know it is about 1,000 years old? Thanks, Wikipedia! I went there recently and got to stand on Charles Darwin. (Well, his gravesite, anyway). At first I was terrified—I was gingerly stepping through the hallway, wondering why this beautiful church would stick gravestones right on the floor, where an average slob like me could step on it. Then I talked to a security guard there who explained that Westminster Abbey was literally packed from floorboard to floorboard with dead people. So about fifteen minutes later I was huffing and puffing my way over dead kings, poets and war heroes. "Wow, that was interesting, that is the person who invented the such-and-such?" Stomp stomp.

Anyway, Prince William (known to many as "Wills") married a commoner, Kate Middleton (I call her "Kates") and they honeymooned in Canada. If you turned on the television during this time, you could not go ten seconds without hearing about the royals touring Canada. Turn on the news—there they are. Turn on a dramatic television show—they would show up during the commercials. Turn on a late-night talk show—celebrities would sit in the chair, and instead of pushing their own book or movie, talk about Wills & Kates! I finally turned off the television, but the force of the Royals was so strong that the TV turned itself back on and pumped out "God Save The Queen" at a volume that quite frankly I found inappropriate (it was 11:00 pm).

Okay not really. But they were on every channel. When they showed up to the Calgary Stampede, people could go see them for free! All they had to do was stand in line for days for a limited number of wristbands. I am guessing either the unemployed, people on vacation, retired people and hobos were front of the line to see Wills & Kates.

I will stop calling her Kates. I never met her so I will remove the last, fictitious "s" from her first name. However, Wills is just too cool a name so I will continue to use it. Wills!

The news even interviewed a Kate "lookalike" who had a similar face and hair. Really? This was news? People died in a burning building, and we have researchers who are working hard to cure diseases, but we won't report on any of that. Here we have someone who looks like someone else. It was either report on this or show a dachshund wearing a hot dog costume. So the news ran with the "royal lookalike" story. She was also wearing a blue dress and declared that while the Royals were in town this week it had been downright crazy! People kept coming up to her and were asking her to get their picture taken with her. This interview was in prime-time and ran for about eight minutes. What a coincidence! I know how she feels—I also happen to look like someone else. I happen to look exactly like the guy who wishes the news channels would actually report on real news.

On parade day, thousands upon thousands of people lined the streets to see the Calgary Stampede parade. Wills & Kate were the marshals of this parade. I am guessing that in addition to being close to the top of the line of succession for the British Monarchy, he also has to make sure that the mascots and juggling clowns on unicycles don't go on some sort of killing spree. Actually, I heard that the royal couple just watched the parade from some comfy seats for about forty minutes. It was probably the weirdest parade ever: people in the actual parade were busy scanning the crowd, eventually screaming "there they are!". The royals were probably waving and shouting at the juggler, "keep throwing the balls in the air. Stop looking at me... do your thing!"

(On an unrelated note: one thing I love about Canadian parades is that you get that one tank rolling down the street, with one or two soldiers poking their heads out. I always wonder who is guarding our county when the entire military is rolling along in the parade. If the Ethiopians ever want to invade, Parade Day is a great day to do it—our one tank is busy that day.)

Not surprisingly, the free wristbands which enabled the hungry public to view these two were all given away within minutes. There was outrage that the people who waited in line could only get two per person. Then some people started selling their free bracelets! Who did these people think they were, charging $100 for a bracelet? People paid this amount, albeit grudgingly, for the chance to stand in a smaller crowd and watch royalty.

How disgusting! I was thoroughly disgusted that these people had made $100 from selling their bracelet and I wasn't one of them. Argh, I should have taken the day off work and made a cool one hundred bones!

Of course, people replied, of course they paid the money. "How else are we supposed to see them?" these people whined. "Where else can we go to see them?" Oh, I don't know. How about turning on the television, to any channel, at any time of day?

Moving

There are two types of people in the world: those who seem to move all the time, and those who live in one house forever. I guess there is a third type of person, known as "those in the third world", but that isn't really funny so we'll just ignore them for the purposes of this essay. I guess there are also people who are on the streets. Again, let's pretend they don't exist. Now that the homeless and the people who live in shantytowns are gone... let the hilarity begin!

We all know someone who has lived in their one-and-only house for their whole lives. Parents, or maybe friends' parents are a great example of the "older generation" who have lived in the same house for decades. You wouldn't even have addresses on these houses. Growing up, you just had "The Johnson's" or "The Smith's" house. That three-level split with the perfect front lawn on the corner? That's the McClure household. The mailman knew them, and you could tell which year they bought their house, because there would be no renovations to it. Ever. The kitchen looked like a 1950s-style kitchen because it was literally purchased in 1958. Never mind that it is 1986 or 1994 or 2006. Who cares! People will walk in during a party and say "wow, you have such a cool 'retro diner' feel to this kitchen!" And the owners, the ancient Mr. & Mrs. Johnson, would nod nervously, hoping no one would notice that sticker on the furnace that says "inspected last on December 12, 1974."

Of course, some of the "live in one house forever" people would actually do renovations. In fact, some super-dads in these homes, knowing that they were never going to move during their lifetimes, were addicted to home improvements. Nothing would ever be good enough for the super-dad. Every year, he would be out in the front yard, standing on the sidewalk and just looking at his house with utter contempt. If you were driving by, all you would see from the street is a bum, the back of a head and some hands on hips. You weren't sure what he was looking at... did his eyes just flicker up to the roof? Is he eyeballing that shrub over in the corner? Yeah, it is probably the shrub. Argh, I hate that shrub so much! And then he would go to the garage and work in there for five hours but never actually build anything. I think I heard a power tool of some kind at one point. What was going on in there?

The other type of person is the "gypsy". I don't know if that is an offensive term. If it is, then you should be ashamed of yourself for reading this book. I mean, come on. You know better—why don't you just put on a white sheet already and go to a Klan meeting!

(Side note: I don't know if gypsies are in any way related to the Klan. I don't think they are. So, you know what? Let's just put aside your hateful view of the world and just enjoy my essay already.)

Where were we? Oh yes, gypsies. (Unless that is offensive, in which case we will call them "little people".) My point is, there are some people that always seem be either moving, getting ready to move, or has just moved. They relax for two weeks and then it is time to move again! Every year, or every spring, or every summer, these people are on the move.

"Hey, when is Penny's housewarming party?"

"It's not happening... she moved again."

"What? I carried a box from her car... I think I just helped her move."

"Move in?"

"Move out... I think."

We all know a Penny. Always on the move. What is the deal with Penny? What is Penny running from? Is that even her real name?

I don't hate these people, these always-moving people. I just don't understand them. I mean, moving is such a chore. It sucks. It is brutal. Every time I have moved, I loudly declare as I am bringing in the last box, sweat dripping from my brow, "I am never moving again!" And then I just sit there on the box and spend about forty-five minutes trying to remember where my toothbrush is.

Never moving again? Fat chance. Life happens and things change, and suddenly you are arriving on the doorstep of some other house, loudly declaring as you bring in the last box, "I am never moving again!" Sigh. Where did I put that toothbrush?

Speaking of boxes: I always wonder what is in that one box. Don't even pretend that you do not know which box I am talking about. You know about that box. I am referring to that one box that sits in your closet, that you have not opened in about twenty years, and yet you move this box around from apartment to apartment, from house to house. You will die of natural causes before that box ever gets unpacked. It's almost like we need that one box to sit there, just to keep us going.

Guy at funeral: It is so sad about Rick. He was so full of life. So sudden. I heard it was his heart.

Wife: No, it was the box. He finally unpacked it.

Guy at funeral: The box from his junior high days? The one with the baseball cards and the copy of the local newspaper from 1987?

Wife: Yep, that was the one. He finally unpacked it. He had no reason to live anymore as that was the last box we had left. It was his time.

Guy at funeral: He was only 38!

Wife: It doesn't matter. He was out of boxes.

The Rodeo

Back in the 1800s, everyone in England wore top hats and the entire world was in black and white. Colour wasn't invented until the 1930s when the Wizard of Oz showed up in movie theatres. Thanks, MGM!

I was recently in England and I stayed in a condo in the same neighbourhood as the London Hospital—this was the place where Joseph (John) Merrick lived in his later years. This was the guy known as The Elephant Man. There was a movie in 1980 about him starring Anthony Hopkins and John Hurt. Great film.

Anyway, my point is this: circuses. The Elephant Man toured with either a circus or a freak show. Can you imagine that in today's time? A touring collection of people who are physically different than us? I know that it happens in some parts of the world in this day and age, but for most of us in the first world, it is distasteful and weird to parade people around and show them off.

There was a form of entertainment back in the 1800s in England called "Bear Baiting". Basically it was a bunch of dogs attacking a bear and people in England sat around and watched it. Good times! Thank goodness it was outlawed in 1835.

The circus certainly is starting to have that feeling these days. Whenever some rinky-dink circus comes through town, there are more and more people protesting it, and less and less people sitting there in the rickety stands eating pink popcorn watching a grizzly bear on roller skates. This is a good thing in my opinion. We should have better things to do than sit around and watch some bear (or any animal) do weird stuff to entertain us. We have television, you know. We no longer need animals performing stunts for us at the circus—not when we can watch Chef Ramsay yell at people trying to make a salad.

I think that the rodeo is up next on the chopping block of "weird" activities that don't really make sense to the younger generation of people. People jump on the backs of bulls and the bulls flail around. We used to secretly cheer for the bulls... man, the guy went flying off! That must have hurt! The difference now is that many people are opening cheering for the bull. They aren't even hiding it anymore. The guy makes his eight seconds without getting his legs crushed and the crowd kind of politely applauds... oh well, there's always the next guy! Maybe he'll get killed. There's always hope!

Cooking

Middle-aged ladies in the office love talking about cooking. Who knew that you could have a heated discussion about rice. Racism? Boring. Poverty? Human rights? Please. Rice is where it is at. There are always one or two ladies in any office who talk about steaming vegetables or they are constantly bringing in cook books. "Hi, can I get this information for the client entered so this company that we all work for can make some profit? No? You are busy talking about Chinese Food and where to buy bulk Won Tons, I understand."

The one day that sticks out in my mind was indeed about the rice. I think we've all been there—it always seems to come back to rice. This was the gist of the conversation that somehow got directed to me as I was heating up some food in the microwave: you must get a rice cooker. I demand it. You have not lived until you have owned a rice cooker. Later in the day I was yelled at about the benefits of rice as I tried to make a photocopy.

You must get a rice cooker, the rice cooker is the greatest, all hail the rice cooker. Well, I am sorry to burst everyone's bubble, but I already have a rice cooker. It is called a pot.

When I explained this, I was greeted with looks of disdain usually reserved for child molesters and people who have sex with corpses. "What? No rice cooker?" I stood my ground. I wasn't going to budge on this one. I finally retorted. What is the big deal with the rice cooker? Can someone please take time out of their busy day not working to explain to me why a rice cooker is the greatest invention ever?"

The answer was simple, if a little mystic: no exploding rice with the rice cooker. The rice just cooks. No exploding.

What? Here is what I want to know: who is exploding rice? How is this a thing? Are you using packets of dynamite to cook the rice? Maybe you are dropping bags of rice on land mines? Where are you cooking dinner, onboard the Hindenburg?

Quickie Oil Changes

The oil change places are so weird. I mean, where else can you just roll your vehicle up to a garage door, and suddenly a little young guy runs out with a coffee and a newspaper? And then you just drive your big rig in there like the King of Siam (if he drove a car) and a small army of serfs start picking away at your vehicle like hyenas on a dead ostrich carcass.

I would love to see this at a restaurant. You are out on a date, and you didn't bother getting dressed up. You and your jogging-pants-wearing significant other waltz into a classy-looking establishment hoping to get a table and a nice meal. Suddenly three young men grab you and your date and proceed to whip off all your clothes, throwing on dressing and tuxedos within two minutes. A comb appears out of nowhere, mouthwash is being guzzled into your mouth and when it is all other, you are looking like a million bucks—and you got to read the sports section during the whole process.

While I respect the oil change business in principle, there is something about it that bugs me. Everything at the oil change is passive-aggressive. I don't like it. The guy comes out—he's usually about sixteen years old and wearing the overalls. So right there, I don't trust him. Yes, I am fully admitting that I am stereotyping someone based on age. When I was sixteen, I was playing with G.I. Joe action figures in the background, and this guy is working on a car? (And when I saying "playing with action figures", what I meant was dating girls. That's what all of us were calling it back in the 1980s. Don't try to verify this part of the story.) The part that I don't like is when the guy comes up to the car and asks me about the oil that they are going to use and the filters that they are going to put in the car. Come on! I literally have no idea what this guy is talking about. He could hold up a jug of maple syrup and I would nod my head. "Sure, that looks really... viscous. Great. I'm reading my free newspaper here. Do anything you want, short of peeing in the gas tank, and I won't know or care." After all, if I knew anything about oil, I wouldn't have waited until the little sticker from the last oil change fell off the inside of the windshield and I started smelling burning french fries coming from under my hood.

So the oil-change professional guy holds up a bottle of the MAX4050 KASTROL MAXIMUM PROFESSIONAL-STRENGTH brand oil, with extra luminescence and quick-action bonding for gears and axels that work in Formula 1 racing cars. Okay... I drive a hatchback and sometimes manage to get up to sixty kilometres an hour before stopping at a red light. Sure, put that in.

"Sir," the guy says, sensing that I am like eighty-five per cent of the world's driving population. "We could use the regular oil that comes in the standard package... or if you truly care about your vehicle, and don't want it to spontaneously combust when you touch the gas pedal, you could consider purchasing the MAXMAX Super Brand 11000 with secret X components. The lunar module and the Mars rover both used this motor oil." Grr. Some people will cave at this point. Some people try to combat this passive-aggressive attitude by explaining why they are choosing the lower-priced option—you know, the one that they came in for?

Oil Clerk: Sir, if you truly care about your vehicle, you should put in the ridiculously expensive oil that they used in the MIR Space Station.

Customer: Well, you see, I've had this car for twenty years. It is literally duct-taped together.

Oil Clerk: It sounds like you really care about this car.

Customer: Boo hoo! Sob, yes, go ahead, I will call my bank and make the financial arrangements.

Back in the old days, oil changes were cheap. Not any more. I'm not falling for that stuff. I am not so soft. The guy mentions the other type of oil and I just play it cool. "I just want the standard package," I say, employing the right combination of smugness and confidence. Well, maybe a bit more smugness than confidence, but you get the idea.

Here's the important part: don't let the army of oil-change workers' derisive stares get you down. They are all judging you. That's fine. That's their job. Well, that and hopefully changing the oil. I can take the heat. I don't know if my car can, because they are putting in some low-grade oil that you wouldn't trust to work a Model T, but we are going for it.

Next up is the filter. I am the master of this. The technician comes back, all shaken and sweaty. They explain that they've just seen something... something horrible! It was black and gooey... what was that thing? Why was it in the car? Often the technician will collapse due to the stress, sobbing uncontrollably into the sales clerk's arms. After all of that:

Oil Clerk: Sir, that black disgusting piece of sludge that looked like a soggy piece of radioactive waste was your air filter.

Customer: Really?

Oil Clerk: What are you doing in this car that is causing your air filter to turn so black? Are you cooking meth in this vehicle?

Customer: Good lord no!

Oil Clerk: Because if you are, you have to tell us. That's the law.

Customer: I am so sorry! I think I ate a hamburger in here once.

Oil Clerk: Sorry? Sorry isn't going to heal the psychological trauma that Jim has suffered. (You may refer to him as "the tech" but he has a name, for the love of all things holy. And a family. He deserves better than this.)

Customer: Wow. I feel awful. What can I do to make up for this?

Oil Clerk: Well, we have a filter that was used in the last Indianapolis 500 and it's only $79.99...

I don't fall for this stuff. Jim the tech can cry, they can show me all the pieces of burnt-toast-that-used-to-be-my-filter they want. The guy shows me my supposed used filter—a black sponge full of ash and cancer—and I just them to put it back in the car. When pressed for how I could be so cruel, I just explain that they are supposed to look that way. Even after only a few days, a normal white filter becomes completely black, oozing with transmission fluid and often has the tail of a small animal sticking out of it.

It doesn't matter if this is true or not. The important thing is that I appear to be confident about it—as if I am certain that this is the truth.

The biohazard team reluctantly reinserts the filter back into the vehicle, tears streaming down their faces. I saw a tech once apologize to the car itself. I could hear the tech murmuring something through the face shield. "I'm sorry... you deserve so much better."

Women have it the worst at these oil change places. If you are a guy, you can kind of fool the oil change people. Now hold on—before everyone starts writing me angry emails or trying to decipher what type of hatchback I drive in an attempt to run me off the highway—I am admitting that I know nothing about cars. I am a big dummy about vehicles. I barely know how to put gas in the tank. I am proud of this. I have a life. And I'm a guy. So that's my point—the oil change companies should be treating us all the same: like idiots. Instead, they treat the women even worse, and to me that is wrong. Yes, I believe in equal rights. While you are nodding and silently wondering if I have received a recent humanitarian award, remember that I will have this exact same view when we are driving around town and the tire falls off. Hey lady, you look as strong as me—why not give it a try? I will be sleeping in the passenger seat if you want some constructive criticism on how that crowbar-thingy works.

My girlfriend went for the oil change once, without me around. The oil change guy said to my girlfriend that he was really torn—he couldn't in good conscience let her drive off the property without doing a complete engine flush—for three hundred dollars! The risk was just too great.

She phoned me and asked if this was really necessary. I told her there was only one way to find out: drive away from the oil change place, and if the car burst into flames, then drive to the nearest hospital emergency room and after the surgery email the service technician an apology.

She was able to wangle the keys back and burned rubber out of there. We found an oil change place that we trust—it is like a doctor or a lawyer. When you find a good one, hold on to it with the firm grip of winter tires on the snowy road.

Aliens

When I was a kid, I loved sitting around in my pajamas watching Star Trek re-runs while I drank cream soda and ate potato chips. Sometimes I would stay up past 10:00 pm! (Okay, confession: all of this actually happened last week—except for the ridiculous part about the pajamas. I always watch TV completely naked.)

Who likes Star Trek? Come on, be honest. Raise your hand! Now please lower your hand, since you are reading a book and I cannot see you. I wouldn't want you embarrassing yourself. Although, if you are a huge trekkie, I doubt that raising your hand is the most embarrassing thing that you have ever done.

Hey, I am not one to judge; I love Star Trek stuff—the original movies, the TV shows, the next show, the one after that, the movies, the other movies... come to think of it, there is a lot of Star Trek. I watched the original series when I was a kid (re-runs) and then my personal favourite was the Next Generation with Patrick Stewart and his band of merry bandits—they Klingon security officer, the android, the psychologist with the spandex jumpsuit...

This pretty much brings me to the point I am trying to make: the female aliens in the Star Trek series are all big-breasted women! It's really perplexing. It's vexing and perplexing. It's almost like the guys who write these science-fiction shows are single guys who figure they have the power to create boobs, right on the printed page!

It always seems like the Enterprise travels thousands of light years to some distant planet in some remote solar system, where the laws of physics have been pushed to their limits through some crazy time-space continuum disaster, and then they meet the alien race who have never had any contact with Earth, or Earthlings, or anything human.

And yet the females have cleavage. And lots of it.

Could this be a universal trait? Could there really be boobies everywhere in the galaxy? Well, scientifically speaking, I think that it is possible, although not probable. It's not even probably probable. It's improbable! Since there is no such thing as an actual alien that the human race has discovered, we have nothing to go on. We have to hypothesize. Worse, we have to use our imaginations. So what do guys think about often? Hmm. It's all starting to make sense now. (Disclaimer: if humans discover aliens after this book goes to print, I am going to be royally pissed. Hopefully we won't make "First Contact" with any race of aliens until after this book has either sold out or recouped any and all set up costs).

Since there are no aliens as of yet, we have to look at other animals on the planet to see if they have cleavage. I've watch a lot of documentaries, Animal Planet network and I've even been to the occasional zoo. Regarding the cleavage: I don't see this happening. I don't think a mammal like a bobcat or an elephant is walking around wearing a bikini or a thong.

Hey, that is okay. That is why it is called science fiction. It wouldn't be much fun to watch Captain Kirk make out with a green alien who looked like a pile of slime. Or a pile of slime wearing a bikini.

Baby On Board

I was driving around town the other day, being my usual productive self (getting a slurpee and getting home as quickly as possible to watch football). I stopped at a red light and noticed that the car in front of me had a big diamond-shaped sign hanging in the rear window. The big, yellow foam sign read

BABY ON BOARD

Okay... baby is inside the vehicle. So now what? I've already stopped at the light. What else am I supposed to do? Normally at any red light, I am sure most of us would just cruise down the street and randomly ram into the car in front of us. Why stop? What's the incentive? And then you see the sign... SCREECH. Thank goodness! There's a baby on board! Save the baby!

Since I drive normally all of the time, regarding of the sign, I am starting to wonder if maybe this foam sign is serving as a reminder to the parents. The doctor at the hospital is looking at the mom and the dad. He just doesn't have a good feeling about these two dummies. "Okay, tell you what," the doctor says. "I'm not entirely convinced that you are going to put the baby inside the car. I saw the ski rack in the parking lot, and quite frankly you look like lazy people. So take this sign, it says 'BABY ON BOARD', and post it in the back of the car." This constant reminder is great for parents. Remember: the baby goes "on board", not up top in the cargo rack!

I wonder if I am supposed to pull up alongside the car with the sign and just start screaming congratulations to them or something. Maybe I pull up at a light and make the old "roll down your window" sign. You know, the "quick hand crank" symbol? Even though no one actually has the old-style windows anymore? But what else do we have? You can't make a "push button" symbol for someone to roll down their window. There's no actually "rolling" anymore. It's all... buzz buzz and down goes the window. There's no buzz buzz sign.

Anyway, I wonder if I am supposed to roll up next to this parent and get him to roll / buzz his window down. Once that happens, I will yell "CONGRATULATIONS, I heard about the baby!" And then if he asks who the hell I am, I'll just point to the diamond sign in the back and yell "I read all about it! Great news!"

I think there should be some sort of sign for people who DON'T have kids. The sign would not be a yellow "caution" or "yield" sign—it would be a big green "GO" sign. The sign would say "NO KIDS ANYWHERE ON BOARD" and upon reading this sign, any of us can go as fast as they want. And stopping at red lights is optional. Hey, this person has no kids, so why bother being safe for the rest of us slobs?

Exercise

Does anyone actually enjoy running on the treadmill? I recently purchased the human-sized hamster wheel because I am going to get in shape. Okay, officially it is a treadmill, but it definitely feels like a hamster wheel. After I run on it I want to sip a Slurpee from a big metal straw from the corner of my cage. The other option, instead of buying a treadmill, was running outside. And I am not going to run outside. Why you may ask?

Well, that is an excellent question. There are a number of reasons, but the biggest one has to be the criminals. Think about it. What if you are out there, going for a jog, loving your life, and suddenly a criminal emerges from the bushes? You are done. It makes sense—either you are running in order to get into shape, which means that you are a big fat flabby out of shape person. If that is the case, you are going to get mugged! Your only possible defense would be to fall on the person and squish him, but since you are running, you are probably not that big. You are big enough to move around and jog, so you aren't "kill a person by falling on them" big. So you will be mugged.

What about skinny people who run? Surely they can't be caught, right? Wrong. In fact, they are the most vulnerable to criminals, because they are already tired. The criminal has been waiting in the bushes for minutes or even hours, probably eating hamburgers or bacon. Maybe he took a nap. Either way, the guy is rested and ready to take your wallet. Skinny people don't stand a chance.

The other big reason that I hate running outside is the weather. It snows, it is windy, there is traffic, and maybe even other runners. What are the rules if two runners are going in the same direction? Do I have to follow the slow guy? For how long? If I am the guy in front, and the other runner passes me, am I allowed to pass them later on? Is this now suddenly a race? Am I a dick for passing the person? What if he mugs me? Too many rules. Not worth it.

So I went out and I purchased a treadmill. The first thing I realized when purchasing any exercise equipment is that the best available option is always

- awesome looking
- has happy people on the box
- ridiculously expensive

The treadmill I was going to buy was the "middle of the road" piece of equipment—it has a track and some lights that light up. Wow. However, once I saw the next treadmill in the line—the PEGASUS ELECTRON 6000 MT with EQUILIBRIUM EXTERIOR and GEL CORE TECHNOLOGY, I knew immediately that I was a loser. I could not in good conscience purchase this other "middle of the road" piece of crap. Sure, they are all essentially the same—they are basically a belt with some grease and wheels, but the PEGASUS ELECTRON 6000 had features that made the other treadmill look like I was literally running on soiled garbage. If I ran on the treadmill outside in the alley, the city's garbage men would insist on throwing it in the big truck and taking it to the dump, even if I was running on it.

The PEGASUS had some crazy bells and whistles. There was some sort of sensor thing that you put on your finger to make sure that you are still registering a pulse while you are huffing and puffing. I am guessing that if you have a heart attack while you are running, not only will the machine turn itself off, but it will guard your finger from the inevitable invasion of mice that will descend on my sweaty dead body. Great. I am saving electricity and saving my dead finger for future generations to marvel at.

I have never seen anyone happy while they are running on a treadmill, ever. So where are they finding this woman on the box? She is running and has a huge grin, her pearly-white teeth illuminating the whole exercise room. "I love running so much!" she is yelling to the photographer. "We're good, we have the picture," he says, but this lady doesn't care. She is in heaven. "I am going to keep running forever!" she yells, her smile getting even wider. Put your finger on the pulse thingy, please, lady. At least she will die happy.

I went home and thought about the differences in the exercise equipment. Some people do yoga to meditate, or maybe they stretch. I sat on the couch with a Slurpee and some Cheezies. I feel that this is the best way to ponder different ways to get in shape. I need all my energy to think.

I made a list of things that I absolutely had to have on the treadmill. Because I get bored by just running, I wanted some place to dock an iPad or a "ghetto blaster", as our generation used to call it. Instead of hooking up my "boom box" with a long extension cord, I could plug in my iPad or iPod or iWhatever into the little slot and my top 30,000 songs would play in a random loop, starting with apparently the most embarrassing songs on there. (Whenever I am playing music in the car I spend a lot of time explaining to the passenger why Boney M or Men Without Hats just seems to keep popping up—stupid Chinese products, the software is all weird).

I think it is also important to have a place to put your water bottle. Have you ever seen those runners at the gym who start on the treadmill by walking one mile an hour? They immediately whip out the water bottle and start guzzling like they have been rescued from a desert island. "It's important to stay hydrated!" they yell while gulping furiously. Yeah, yeah, we get it. The only fluids they are replacing are those lost from spittle as they are yelling to their friend about what happened on television the other night. If you are talking, it means that you are not running fast enough!

When I run, I run. I go at a pretty good speed. I like to make it interesting, so I either listen to music, watch the iPad, or just pretend that the authorities are chasing me. In fact, that would be a great app to put on the exercise machines: the LAM 9000. Be on the LAM! The exercise program would be a little digital criminal (maybe wearing striped pajamas and a mask? I'm just spitballing here) and the police and their dogs give you a three minute head start. You are on the treadmill, and you can slow down if you want—that is, if you want your digital criminal to be eaten by hungry dogs! That would be a fun game. Occasionally you would have to jump over a digital hedge or pretend to scale a fire escape.

The last level would be you as a digital criminal hiding in the bushes. When you start running, he jumps out and you get to chase a runner who is foolishly running outside. If you catch him, you get to digitally beat him up and take his wallet.

Anyway, I bought the "middle of the road" treadmill, and it is doing a great job of keeping the hardwood flooring pinned down in the exercise room. I'm pretty sure the doctor said that I am supposed to get cardiovascular exercise two to three times per year, and it is only October, so I have a couple of months yet. Right now I am mentally preparing first: in my mind, I am hiding in the bushes.

Things I Hate About Christmas

Don't get me wrong. I do actually enjoy some things about Christmas. They say it is better to give than receive—and it does my heart joy to see the happy looks on my friends' faces as I open up my gifts. I am really glad I can help them out.

We now live in an age with the dreaded gift card. Remember the good old days, when grandma used to just put a fresh twenty in your Christmas card? That sucker used to go through the mail! Nowadays, that is completely unacceptable. Sending cash through the mail is probably the number-one way that terrorist organizations get their funding. I am guessing that they basically steal mail, open it up, take out all the twenty-dollar bills, and then buy brand-new monkey bars. (I've seen the footage on CNN. Those monkey bars are nice.)

So cash is out. No one uses cash anymore. Even stores don't like taking some cash. Liquor stores always have a big sign in the window "less than $50 on site". Well, the last guy just bought two skids of beer, and I don't think he was paying with deer pelts. So that cash has to be somewhere in the store.

Stores don't like taking old money either. Canada and the United States keep changing their money around—new paper, new faces on the bills, more holograms. If you have a twenty dollar bill that is more than six months old, I suggest you get to a Wal-Mart as soon as possible and buy something, anything.

Money is out. Cash is out. It is all gift cards now. People apparently love the gift cards—it is just like cash, only more restrictive. It is like an adult-to-adult allowance. I remember when I was eight years old, and I mowed the lawn for my parents. It was hard, grueling work, trying to figure out how to get out of doing the yard work. Finally I gave up and just mowed the lawn. When I was done, my parents gave me a crisp fiver. My eyes dilated like a cat when they see a bird wandering around the front yard. I had big plans with that five dollars: I was going to the 7-Eleven and getting high on slurpee and chips. Do you ever see those homeless guys downtown, all strung out on drugs? They are just sitting there, stoned out of their minds, not moving, just hanging out on the curb watching the world go by. There is no difference between that scenario and eight-year-old boys sitting in front of the 7-Eleven drinking grape Slurpees.

My dad, however, had other ideas regarding my recent wealth. "You should at least save some of that money!" he would say, looking both stern and happy. He was stern because he was a dad, but he was happy because he now had low-cost child labour for general contracting and landscaping. I had proven that I could operate a lawn mower for a half hour without chopping off a foot.

Christmas carries that kind of authoritative restrictive giving to the extreme. It's like going to the mall with a wound-up energetic guy—he wants to buy you a gift, but it has to be exactly correct. You are now hanging out with obsessive-compulsive guy at the mall. Enjoy your gift card! It is for this store only! Don't even think about going into those other stores. Don't even look in that direction! This store, right here!

The gift card is just one of the many things I hate about Christmas as well. Remember Paul McCartney? He used to be a Beatle, which means that anyone over the age of forty pretty much considers him the closest thing to Superman or Jesus that we have right now.

I like Paul McCartney. He's great. But I can't take "Simply Having A Wonderful Christmastime" anymore. I'm done with it. I have heard it in the mall, every Christmas season, for the past thirty years. As soon as I hear the first notes—the synthesized "bing bong bing bong" my stomach turns. Enough! Society has been around for ten thousand years—can we crank out ten other Christmas songs to at least keep things fresh at the mall?

I am joking of course—there are in fact other Christmas songs, but I don't like them either. John Mellencamp has that creepy "I Saw Mommy Kissing Santa Claus" song. I get it now, as an adult. Santa Claus is really dad in a red suit. That makes sense to me. But when I was seven years old, I didn't understand that Santa was my dad. So when I heard that mommy was making out with Santa Claus, it was a little bit disturbing. Why is mommy doing that with this stranger? Are other mommies doing this as well? Santa visits millions of homes on Christmas Eve. Is he banging all these chicks and dropping off toys? It just gets creepier and creepier.

Nice work, Mellencamp.

I figured out that Santa wasn't real eventually—I don't remember exactly when, but I was still young enough to visit "Santa" at the mall. I sat on his lap and looked at his face—his glasses, his big white beard. And then I noticed that his arms had bright red hair on them. Hmm. I was about eight years old. Something seemed weird. I had no internet back then, so I just pondered it for a few weeks leading up to Christmas. The wheels were turning. How could one guy visit millions of homes in one night? Even with the time changes, it seemed a little unlikely.

And why was Santa's workshop making toys? I received a Matchbox car and a Hasbro game. Was Santa making these? Were they counterfeit products? Some elf was banging them out in the factory, making them for all the little boys and girls all around the world, and then stamping them Milton Bradley or Mattel? It didn't seem fair to the companies. Was there a licensing deal? Were these giant corporations using slave labour to create more products around the holidays? The whole thing just seemed fishy to me.

And you mean to tell me, that three weeks before Christmas, when Santa is arguably at his busiest time of year in regards to production and quotas, that he's hanging out a the mall? And not just any mall in the world—my mall, in my neighbourhood? How is that even remotely plausible? Aren't you busy? You mean to tell me that your staff are so motivated and organized that you don't need to supervise them on a workday twenty days before you have to deliver all these gifts. Come on.

By the way, I would love a train set. I'm just telling you this now? Three weeks before Christmas? If I was Santa, I would have a deadline six-months prior to Christmas. Get your order in by June 30th. That's the deadline. Hey, your parents know how to file their taxes—they can send me a note telling me that you want a Barbie doll.

Things We Are Embarrassed About—But Shouldn't Be

The nice thing about a book is that you can read in silence about all sorts of weird stuff that you would normally not want anyone else to know you are looking at. It is more difficult to watch a movie or a television show about a medical condition—oh, look at that! They are operating on that poor guy! There's blood everywhere! But you can read all about that same procedure and you look like a smarty pants.

There are definitely some things that people should be ashamed of. For example, if you are spending your free time beating up old people or lighting cats on fire, then shame on you. I think most of us can agree that these people should be embarrassed. However, we have all been embarrassed, ashamed and even mortified over things that—well, when you think about it, aren't really that big of a deal.

Hemorrhoids

This is one that I can't figure out. According to the National Digestive Diseases Information Clearinghouse, seventy-five per cent of people at some point in their lives will get hemorrhoids. (I am pretty sure I would not want to get a letter from Digestive Clearinghouse. I may already be a winner—if winning means I have blood in my stool.) Seventy-five per cent? That seems like a really high number. Apparently, according to science, hemorrhoids are caused by straining when we go to the bathroom. Okay, well I am going to go out on a limb here and say that approximately one hundred per cent of the world goes to the bathroom in some way.

There are basically two types of people in the world:
1. People who take magazines and books into the bathroom
2. People with stuff to do

I am proud to say that I am in the second group. I don't have three hours to kill, leafing through Reader's Digest and learning about a bear attack in the Rocky Mountains or how to make a cake out of licorice nubs and green food colouring. I have actual stuff to do during the day. When I go to the bathroom, I go in there with a plan. I do my business and then I leave. It's like a bank robbery—you get in, you make a deposit, then you get out. Okay, I guess you make a withdrawal. Either way, my point is that I'm not spending any more time in the washroom then I have to. I leave. Quickly. It sounds to me like hemorrhoids are badges of honour that you are living life with a purpose instead of hanging out in bathrooms for hours.

Condoms

This one is really weird when we think about it. There are two seventeen-year dudes hanging outside the drug store. One is getting ready to have hot, sweaty sex with his girlfriend. He needs some condoms. Right now. The other guy is going home and watching television and hoping to see a boobie on the late-night movie. So why is the sex guy the one who should be embarrassed?

Do you have any idea how hard (pardon the pun) it is to get laid in high school? Oh sure, we see it in the movies all the time—Fast Times At Ridgemont High, American Pie, and the critically-acclaimed Ski Lodge 7: Attack of the Women's Volleyball Team. People in high school are gettin' naked and gettin' it on. The van is a rockin' and don't come-a-knockin'. However, real life is not that glorious. Have you ever cross-examined the one kid in high school who says that he was screwing all day and all night? If you start digging for the truth, you might find that he actually felt around in the dark and wound up with something that he is going to his grave believing was a nipple.

That having been said, some people are in fact having sex—you can look at teen moms. There are young ladies who are in high school right now and they are pregnant (or just had a baby). So this means that someone, somewhere during their high school years was getting busy. So it means that one of the following has to be true:

1. A guy going to high school had a good time for twenty to twenty-five seconds

2. There are some seriously creepy old guys hanging around high school

3. Aliens are real and they have probes!

My point is this: if a guy goes into the store and wants to buy some condoms, I say good for him—at least he is trying to not get the girl pregnant. He should be applauded for both the responsibility that he is taking on, plus the fact that some girl is willing to see him naked, even if it is with the lights off.

Farting

How many times have you been in the office, quietly making photocopies, and suddenly it smells like death? Or maybe burnt macaroni and blueberry yogurt? Chances are very high that Richard in accounting walked by about ten seconds earlier? I thought so.

People are terrified of farting in all sorts of places—crowded elevators, the big meeting at work, the church, your parole hearing, etc. Well guess what? According to every fart I have ever smelled, one hundred per cent of the public lights it up once in a while. It is completely natural.

Yes, it stinks. But guess what? All sorts of things stink. What about the person at work who insists on microwaving her tuna casserole for five minutes, even though her colleagues are praying for a meteorite strike? What about the bicycle-riding guy who shows up to work sweaty? I love this guy. He comes in the door wearing the spandex. Now he has to change. He's saving the environment and getting a workout, but he's twenty minutes late to the meeting and smells like me on the weekend. He might refuse to use any deodorant because he doesn't want to get lymph-node cancer. Well, guess what. I am pretty sure that showers do not cause any cancer whatsoever. I think water is medically cleared. If you don't have a shower at work, you should not be allowed to ride your bike to work. You also shouldn't be allowed to run to work—in fact, walking quickly in the halls should be discouraged. If I was the boss, I would keep the thermostat at sixty degrees Fahrenheit and be on the constant prowl throughout my office for any visible beads of sweat. The people who spend their days eating calamari or doing lunch-time yoga without showering need to be embarrassed, not fart-guy. Fart-guy is digesting food properly. That's a good thing. Does it smell like barbeque chicken wings and avocado?   Absolutely. Did you ask to smell it? Absolutely not. But we can all just pretend that it is normal, can't we?

Actually, come to think of it, maybe there are a few things we should be embarrassed about—but only if we can't blame it on the other guy standing in the elevator.

10,000 Feet: I Jumped

People always whine about their "bucket list"—things to do before they die. I'm among these whiny whiners—if you are sitting by me at a cocktail party, chances are good that you will hear me moaning about not going to the Taj Mahal or not having thrown someone through a plate-glass window in a bar fight. Yet. However, I am proud to announce that I actually knocked something off the bucket list: I jumped out of a perfectly good airplane at 10,000 feet.

I've always wanted to parachute at least once—well, I say "always", but really it was ever since watching Band of Brothers and watching the Allies jump out of the airplanes over Normandy. Hey, D-Day looks cool! Well, not the whole "getting shot at by Nazis" but the other parts looked pretty cool.

I got given an awesome Christmas gift—a day of skydiving—so we were off to Sin City Skydiving in Las Vegas.

We met up with the van at Bally's and signed our 14-page waiver. It says something along the lines of:

SKYDIVING IS A DANGEROUS ACTIVITY THAT CAN RESULT IN SERIOUS INJURY AND DEATH. I ACKNOWLEDGE THIS AND WON'T SUE ANYONE.

Have a great time Skydiving!

Good times. All aboard!

The skydiving place was located about forty minutes outside of Las Vegas, right next to what looked at a Nevada Corrections Center. This made sense to me—our chain gang of six people on the bus were quiet and somewhat remorseful as we rolled off the highway and past the prison. We stopped at the rinky-dinky airport. I expected to see a warden standing there, chewing tobacco and explaining to us that we weren't in "the world" anymore.

I have to pull out the full disclaimer: this was a tandem jump, which means that some other guy is doing all the work while I am just hanging there like a baby kangaroo at the zoo. Which, by the way, is fine by me. A couple people have said "doesn't it bother you to be strapped on to a dude"? Not in the slightest. For me, this is the only circumstance in Las Vegas where fully-clothed, big, strong guy is way better than little bikini lady.

The skydiving staff were awesome—I used my joke for the one hundredth time on these guys and they pretended to laugh. (The joke was "my Christmas gift is jumping out of an airplane, and my girlfriend's Christmas gift is throwing me out of the airplane." The joke killed with tourists at Caesar's Palace, the Bellagio, and the hot dog guy outside of Bill's Gambling Hall.)

There were six of us total, but only four of us were jumping. The other two were "watchers"—friends or family, standing there and worrying. If you ever want to second-guess yourself before jumping out of an airplane, listen to these people. They are coming up with all sorts of logical and completely rational reasons why I am in idiot. Don't listen to them! You are the big show and besides, there are no refunds.

There were four clients, and two clients (strapped to two professionals) go up together in one plane ride. I was in the second group. So I had a half hour to sit on a couch, listen to Iron Maiden play out of the ghetto blaster and watch some stranger fold a parachute. I have to say, the guy knew how to pack a chute. It was like a reverse clown car. Big chute, little chute, littler pack. I need this guy on vacation to pack my suitcase. Unfortunately, my girlfriend became my caddy, and I used my nervous energy to constantly inquire about the status of my ball cap, wallet, ball cap, and wallet. Do you have my wallet? WHERE'S MY WALLET? I switched gears at one point and asked about the passport. Do you have my passport? WHERE IS IT? (It was back at the hotel and at that point I was encouraged to take a walk around the building.)

Finally the plane landed, they unloaded, everyone popped inside the building looking happy and I was teamed up with Mike, also known as the guy who knew what the hell was going on. All hail Mike! I put on a green one-piece jumpsuit, which instantly made me feel like an astronaut. Mike had on a helmet. Great. I looked around for my helmet.

There was no helmet. Mike got the helmet.

I did wonder a little why Mike got some head protection but I was going to be flapping in the wind. Oh well. Details! I was told a bunch of stuff about what was going to happen but I stopped paying attention after "terminal velocity of 130 miles per hour". I guess that if at that point the chute didn't open, I would just bend with the knees and everything would be fine.

I strutted out to the airplane, which was really just a glorified go-kart with wings. They had removed all the seats and covered the screws with duct tape, so it looked like the result of me trying to make an airplane in the back yard. We crawled in to the back and a little plastic rickety door closed. This thing was rattling and shaking as we took off. I loved it! It was also really loud—the quarter-inch thick PVC door wasn't really really soundproofing the engine.

It was an awesome twenty-minute airplane ride up to 10,000 feet. I was sitting in-between Mike's legs facing away from him. I could feel him tugging at ropes and levers and pulleys, checking that everything was okay. I am a big fan of this. Keep tugging. You do what you need to do. He pointed out some cool sights like the MGM Grand in the distance and a really neat solar farm near the California border. Wow! I was okay with the describing, but I needed to continue to feel some tugging. Keep checking!

Twenty minutes is just long enough to lull you into a false sense of security. Hey, it's just a plane ride! I was looking around, enjoying life, and wondering when drinks were going to be served. Mike ordered me to sit right on him and he linked us together super tight. People will ask me "wasn't that weird?"

Well, he opened the airplane door and everything changed. Suddenly my legs were dangling outside of the aircraft and I was looking out at the world. It was freezing, incredibly loud and windy. So was it weird that I was tethered to Mike? Hell no! At this point I was ready to crawl inside his belly button if it was allowed.

We rolled out the door and plummeted to Earth. The free fall was about thirty seconds and it was absolutely ridiculous. My adrenaline gland was squeezed like a rag getting hand-washed by a peasant. We reached terminal velocity, which is the fastest that you can fall (because the air offers resistance equal to the force of the falling). We were dropping like a rock, and I screamed but no sound came out. I am pretty sure that bending my knees would not have saved me at this point.

The chute opened and suddenly everything was calm. It felt like we weren't even falling! It was really quiet (we could use regular speaking voices) and Mike asked me if we wanted to do some spins and like an idiot I said hell yes!

We were spinning in circles right above a highway and some power lines and loving every second of it. I started getting a little nauseous after the twelfth spin so I was kind of glad that the ground was coming up fast. We slowly approached the landing zone and Mike instructed me to lift my legs, because we were going to land on my bum. Well... yeah, I don't actually have a bum. I'm what's medically known as "puny" or "wimpy". I have bony-bum condition. So at the last minute I timed it just right so I scraped the ground with my feet and kind of sat/stumbled onto the ground. Remember I had mentioned that the airplane carried two clients? Yeah I forgot about that too. So about five seconds later the other jumper (a lovely lady from New York) landed in the other part of the landing area. We were alive, we were alive!

We went back to the hotel where we were staying and hung out in the Tex-Mex restaurant by the casino. We had a couple of drinks. I can honestly say I did not feel "scared" in the sense that I was going to die.

Fast forward about two weeks later. I'm online and for some strange reason, I felt a huge compulsion to type into the search engine "tandem instructor passed out". Could such a thing even happen?

I totally recommend googling this after you have skydived. Don't do it before. It's kind of like when you are getting ready to eat stinky mussels or squid. The general advice seems to be "just close your eyes and eat it! Don't think too much!" Well, the same can be said about tandem instructors passing out. I read an article about a regular guy who was taking his first tandem jump. Hey, that sounds just like me! His experience was a little different. They jumped out of the airplane, and their chute opened—woo hoo! The first-timer was loving life!

Then the tandem instructor (the professional who knew what he was doing) had a heart attack and passed out.

So now buddy the tourist has gone from having a great memory to pretty much just a memory at this point. The first-time jumper, the tourist, was a military guy, so he apparently had some instinct that involved reaching up over the now-deceased instructor and working the ropes to land safely, even though he had never done that before, and if he misjudged the pulling of the ropes he still could have landed way too quickly and killed himself.

Did I feel inferior yet? Yes, yes I did. The tourist/military guy landed, and then somehow worked himself free of the tandem straps and then performed CPR on the instructor! Come on. I couldn't even have told you where the rope was located. I would have reached back and grabbed hair, that was about it.

Tourist guy/military guy is definitely a superhero. Unfortunately, the instructor didn't survive, but I think we can all agree that the first-timer guy should be given the army title Major Awesome. The first-time tandem guy said that he is never jumping again. I can't say that I blame him. You are never going to forget that awful day.

You never know how you will react in a stressful, life-and-death situation, but I can guarantee that I would not have done that. I have no such rope-pulling skills, and pretty much would be a useless lump on the way down. I would think I would be worse than a lump, because I would be screaming and crying and probably peeing as well. So if you are ever out for a walk in your neighbourhood on a bright sunny day, and suddenly you hear screaming from up above, do not look up and stare at the clouds with your mouth open.

New Year's Resolutions Are Dumb

Okay, so here is some free advice regarding your new year's resolutions. Yes I am a giver. (Okay maybe it is not free if you bought the book. So consider this already-paid for advice. Either way, you are getting it.)

You might be reading this well-crafted book in the bathtub or on a train. I have no idea. However, I do know one thing: eventually, inevitably, the Christmas season will show up. And it will be followed by the New Year's season. Christmas season is like the house party. Yay, Christmas is here! Have some fudge! What do you mean, you "shouldn't"? Didn't you just jump out an airplane? You should be dead. Have some damn fudge.

New Year's Eve, on the other hand, is like when the house party gets to midnight and grandma has left and now it is just hot chicks and rap music. No one is quite sure what is going on, everyone who is forty or older is home asleep, and the booze, cigarettes, alcohol and partying is in full swing. Happy New Year! It's midnight, you have to kiss someone, that is the law.

New Year's Day follows. Blah. It is literally the morning after. You look out the window, ask yourself if this year feels any different, remind yourself four or five times that the next time you write a cheque you need to have a different number at the end of the year, and then you feel shame.

This New Year's holiday, let's all take a moment to reflect on how horrible we are as human beings. We've had enough! It's time to make some resolutions. This will be the year that we finally get our act together and lose the pounds, stop the smoking, the drinking, the bad habits, and finally do something worthwhile with our lives. Okay, okay... we all know it is a lie, but we still make the resolutions anyway. Why is it so difficult for some people to make new year's resolutions? Actually, making the resolution is easy—it is keeping them that seems to be so difficult. After all, you have one day to make the resolution, and then 364 days or so to continue eating cheezies on the couch while watching Wheel of Fortune. That's a lot of Wheel. Of. Fortune!

Well, fear not promise-maker. I have the answer. I have decided that instead of making New Year's resolutions that are going to be impossible to carry through on, such as exercise and eating properly, I will just make some New Year's resolutions based on things that I don't do anyway. That's the key. You look like a hero even though you aren't actually doing anything differently. No one has to know!

Resolution: No more armed robberies.
You know what? It just isn't fun anymore. The guns, the frightened people... it isn't worth it. Sure, I was banking $100,000 cash a week, but was I really happy?

Resolution: No more dumping toxic waste into the river.
It was kind of cool the first few years I did it, but quite frankly, it is becoming more of a habit than anything I actually "enjoy" doing. It's easier to just bury the huge barrels of radioactive plutonium in the yard. Plus the drive out to the lake is just getting too crowded, what with the children playing and the people fishing for the mutant trout that now swim in the lake.

Resolution: Always wear clothing at the office.
This one will be tough to stick to but I just need to realize that not everyone wants to see me do data entry with no shirt on. I might still wear the housecoat and slippers on casual Fridays, but we'll take that on a week-by-week basis.

Resolution: I will let the police do their job.
Yes, a few weekends a year I like to drive around with a police scanner and show up at the scene of a crime. And then solve the crime. It's just something I've done ever since watching CSI. It's kind of "my thing". I get just as much fun out of finding "the real killer" as I do whipping off my sunglasses and yelling "YAAAAAAAAAAAAAA" in the Roger Daltrey voice.

Playing Jeopardy At Home

I am slowly turning into my dad. This shouldn't be a surprising thing to anyone who is already super old, because they have already turned into their parents. But, for someone like me, who is not quite an old man yet, it is a bit shocking. I find myself watching PBS shows on television. Sometimes when I drive around in my car, I will find myself listening to talk radio. I used to be that guy who was rocking out to The Who and Pink Floyd, and now I am listening to a radio interview about planting geraniums in the spring? Help me!

I generally hate game shows—I kind of think they are stupid. I mean, why is everyone so excited all the time? A guy dressed up as a hot dog is told to "come on down!" and suddenly they are spinning a huge wheel or guessing who is behind curtain number three. (Okay, I admit, I might be combining a few game shows to create a hybrid-ultra-dumb game show.)

My favourite is when the contestant is playing on some game show and the amount they are winning is ridiculously small. "Okay, Mary, this next question is for three point!" Ooooh. Three whole points! The grand prize winner has twenty points! Wow! They are like the Bill Gates of points.

I do, however, watch one game show: Jeopardy. This show is nerd central. I love it. The people on this show aren't just smart—they are super smart. They are the people at the cocktail parties just standing there sneering at regular idiots like me and sadly asking "you didn't know that? Yes, Uzbekistan and Liechtenstein are doubly-landlocked, although of course that didn't happen until after World War I. Can you pass the hor d'oeuvres? Do you know what that word means?"

I really like Jeopardy. It is fun to watch. However, it is really, really fun to play with another person.

My girlfriend and I like to play Jeopardy, but I totally admit that the reason we enjoy playing is that we are both super competitive.

Quick story: shortly after I met my girlfriend, we decided to go out for dinner during the week. That evening, I had a recreational soccer game that I had already committed to. I was playing goalkeeper for a rec division "C" team. Rec "A" is the really good players; Rec "B" are the older players who can't quite move as fast, or maybe some players who are not that skilled; Rec "C" is where they put the rest of us. If you can tie up your cleats, you passed the test and are able to play in Rec "C".

We were up 4 to 1 at halftime and my girlfriend showed up. Alright, I was pumped up! We had a three goal lead and I could showboat a little bit and impress the lady. Well, that quickly changed when we let in a bunch of goals and wound up losing the game 6 to 5. When I say "we" let in a bunch of goals, I admit, I was the goaltender. Have you ever goaltended in soccer? The net is way too large. It is annoying. Needless to say, we lost and I was angry. Because we were going out for dinner, I now found myself angry and hungry—not a great combination. I got in the car and pretended to be happy.

"Oh well," I lied, "I guess it just wasn't our night."

"What are you talking about?" she said. "You guys stunk! What a collapse!"

"Yes!" I screamed. Now we are talking! Here was someone who really understood me. We spent the evening eating food and yelling about how awful the soccer collapse was.

This brutal, unrelenting competitiveness is great when playing Jeopardy at home. Here is a quick recap of the rules:

1. Get a pen and a paper.

2. You can't shout out an answer until Alex is done talking. If you jump the gun, then you can either forfeit the point, or you can just get yelled at—whatever is more fun for the other person.

3. If you correctly shout out the answer (and the other person doesn't), score one point. It doesn't matter if the question is the first one or the last one, a big money value or a little money value—they are all worth one point.

4. When one of the contestants on the television gets the daily double, you still guess—but if you get it correct, you score two points. This really chokes the other person if you get this one!

5. When you get to Final Jeopardy, you can bet up to the full value of your points. Usually I chicken out and bet a whopping one or maybe two points.

6. You can play all five games during the week, and then the winner of the week is the person with the most points at the end of day Friday. It is a great feeling knowing that one of you will be in a foul mood heading into the weekend. Good times.

How To Spot A Lazy Co-Worker

This book isn't just a series of essays where I complain. No. You get your money's worth right here. I'm about to share a little piece of advice that might save you a ton of time, energy and sanity.

There are many lazy co-workers out there. Hell, they are probably in your office right now—especially if it is between the hours of 10:00 am and 2:00 pm. (They tend to show up late and leave early). Usually, lazy co-workers are pretty easy to spot, if you know where to look.

Example #1: Ask for help. Do you need help carrying a box of paper back to the printer? Suddenly Jerry in accounting has developed a ruptured disc in his spine, or possibly Ankylosing spondylitis, which is a chronic inflammation of the axial skeleton. Thanks for the help, Jerry! If pressed for details, Jerry will either gladly spend forty seconds to produce medical evidence (prescriptions, x-rays, medical receipts) or he will claim that such a demand is a "violation of his privacy". Good ol' Jerry. He has the energy to Google a spinal condition but can't lift a box. What a bum.

Example #2: Coffee. This only works if your suspected lazy co-worker likes to drink coffee. Go over to the coffee pot and just pour the whole thing down the sink. Now, you can do one of two things. The first strategy is to just hide behind a potted plant or under your desk. Simply and wait for the co-worker to eventually go get a cup of coffee. When he sees that the pot is empty, they will either
•throw their head back in disgust and go back to their desk (lazy)
•make another pot (not lazy)
However, this strategy has some risks. The most obvious one is that some other co-worker could show up and simply make some more coffee. That is no good. You are running a sting operation

here people! The other pitfall is that your boss will come by at the exact wrong time and see you pouring perfectly good coffee down the drain and then leave like a psychopath.

The other, and quite frankly more dangerous risk is that you could be hiding under your desk for two or three hours. That would make you technically lazy, thus defeating the purpose of the whole operation. So I would caution you to hide under your desk (or in the plant) for a maximum of three to five minutes, and definitely pretend that you are looking for a contact lens if the president happens to spot you peeking out like a scared rabbit from behind the ficus tree.

There is an alternative to hiding under your desk or behind the plant. Dump the coffee and then ask the co-worker to make some more. They could do one of three things:

1. Claim they don't know how (lazy)
2. Get up and help you (not lazy)
3. Ask if your hands are broken, or if you forgot how to use the water faucet

The third question can sting—especially if there are other co-workers around. Again, I never promised that this would be easy.

Example #3: Tell a story. Okay, this is the best strategy, because you will get an answer relatively quickly and it won't involve dumping coffee and claiming that you have no idea how indoor plumbing works. Here is the plan: start up a casual conversation with your suspect. Maybe ask them where they went to school, how they liked it, et cetera. Then, without warning, you spring the trap.

Ask them about group work.

You could do it like this:

You: Hey there, Bob from accounting, how's it going?

Bob: Hello. I'm Bob.

You: Yes, yes you are. How's it going?

Bob: I work in accounting.

You: Personality plus. So Bob, where did you go to school?

Bob: I earned a BFCA with honors at the Johnston Institute of Nerdology in the beautiful state of Oregon. I then took at five-year accounting diploma degree—

You: I'm going to stop you there before I find a window and jump. So, in your school, did you like group work?

The suspect will have only one of two reactions, and you can instantly ascertain their work ethic:

1. They loved group work! (lazy lazy lazy)
2. They will instantly get a pained look on their face and start glancing around nervously for a wastepaper basket. They will grab it and loudly vomit into the basket. (not lazy)

The only downside to this strategy is that if there is no wastepaper basket nearby, you might get wet.

This strategy overall is sound. Any of us who have ever done group work know about the "slacker" member of the group. Slackers love group work, since they can spend their time eating chips on the couch, while the rest of us are busy researching, compiling, meeting, debating with our classmates and trying to actually pass the class. I think we've all been there—the one piece of the project that you asked slacker to do, they haven't "had time" to get accomplished. But hey, if watching Jerry Springer and sleeping in until 10:00 am every day was a class, they would get an A-plus!

This lazy mentality is all fine and dandy in high school or university, because we don't have a choice about things in school. We have to do whatever the teacher wants. However, at work... actually, come to think of it, work is pretty much the exact same way—we just have to do whatever the boss wants. Hmm—well, let me say this then: it is better to know in advance who the lazy co-workers are, so that when you are eventually teamed up with them on the big project, and you are forced to do all the work, at least you can take satisfaction in knowing in advance that they were lazy bums.

It's all about the small victories.

And, if they are not a lazy co-worker, at least you get to watch someone throw up in a wastepaper basket.

Giving Blood: What Really Goes On

If I am going to call this book a "self help" book, it means that at some point I have to stop being hilarious and start actually handing out some advice. And it can't just be "don't eat yellow snow" (although that is always good advice, especially north of the 49th parallel. There is lots of snow up there, and lots of dogs everywhere).

I am proud to announce that I have given blood more than thirty times. Thirty bloods. Thank you, thank you. And I will add: voluntarily, too! Yes, poking my hand with a fork does not count. Here is how it all began:

The NBA basketball playoffs were on back in the mid-2000s, and I was sitting on the couch like a lazy bum. I might have had a slurpee and/or a bag of barbeque chips—the details are a bit fuzzy and unfortunately lost to history forever. However, I do remember a basketball player getting interviewed. I think he played for the Denver Nuggets or San Antonio Spurs. I am just at this point realizing that I have turned into a senior citizen and am revealing details that no one really cares about. Tighten it up Wiebe! Okay, so this millionaire basketball player had met a young kid at one of the millionaire basketball practices. The kid was really ill and needed a bone marrow transplant. The kid was talking with the basketball player, and he basically said that if he received the bone marrow transplant, he could go on to live a relatively normal life, but if he didn't get the bone marrow transplant, he would probably die.

The basketball player was stunned and put a call out to the people of Denver. Or San Antonio. The important part: go get tested! Maybe you could be the person who could save this kid's life! Well, the people of the city responded and turned out in droves to get tested.

It turned out that some guy in the Denver area (or San Antonio area) was a match and the kid was saved. Great story, halftime is over, back to the slurpee and chips!

Well, I figured it was about high time I did something other than just root for Michael Jordan. (I was cheering against whatever team had the basketball player who saved the kid's life. Does that make me a bad person?) I went downtown a few days later and was a first-time blood donor. (That should even it out.)

First of all, what I love about giving blood is that every volunteer in there usually says "wow, thanks for coming in!" Many people would call me cheap, frugal, or possibly really cheap, so I am not a big fan of donating money. I am always afraid that the big corporate fat cats are going to not spend it wisely. Hey, those charity commercials on television cost money and somebody is paying for it. However, I have no problem donating my time or blood. I'm just sitting in a chair and letting my heart do something it is already doing anyway—pumping blood! Now that is my kind of charitable work right there. If there is a way that I can help those in need while at the same time take a nap, sign me up.

So it starts off by showing up and getting some literature. The receptionist gives me a number (a laminated square with a number 35 on it) and then some pamphlet about mad cow disease or something. I always say that I read the pamphlet but really I am just sitting in the little reception area watching the flat-screen television that some organization donated to the blood services place. Hey, here is an idea: if you want us to read the depressing pamphlet about mad cows or whatever the disease is called, then turn off a guy with a megaphone yelling at people who are trying to build a house for a family of eight in just seventy two hours. I don't care how mad the cow is, you just can't compete with entertainment like that.

Even though I made an appointment, I have to wait for my name to be called for two or possibly three minutes. What? Don't they know who I am? Instead of the logical reaction, which would be to get outraged, berate the staff and leave in a huff, I pass the time by taking a complimentary can of Coke, popping the top and just guzzling that bad boy down. Not only is this charitable endeavor not costing me any money, but after the can of soda, I figure I'm up on the whole trip about sixty to seventy cents right there.

I get up to the little medical station and the lady asks me which finger I want to get poked with a needle. Which finger do I want to get poked? Is this a trick question? They do this to test for iron.

My attitude is that if I can make it out of my chair and over to the finger-poking station without fainting, chances are pretty good that I am ready to give blood. The nurse isn't buying it. They prick my finger and that is the worst part. It stings for a couple of seconds. I tough it out by remembering that Ghandi probably never gave blood. I'm guessing his iron was too low (what with the hunger strikes and stuff). I'm not saying specifically that I am better than Ghandi—we are both awesome in our own way.

The computer reads the blood droplet and it has been determined that my iron levels are "passable". I guess licking the inside of the can of beans has finally paid off after all. The ridicule was worth it.

Next up: the questionnaire. I sit at what looks like a little voting station and they have a pen with a big chain attached to it. They're handing out Coke and cookies like they can't get rid of groceries fast enough, but there are only three pens in the whole building. I read through the questions—they are simple enough but designed to weed out the suspicious people in our society.

"Do you feel well today?" Why, yes... yes I do! I passed the iron test, I'm full of Coca-Cola and I haven't vomited blood even one time today.

"Have you taken any drugs today?" and the list goes on and on. It's pretty common stuff—basically they want to make sure that I am not a walking zombie ready to make someone else ill with my blood. That makes sense.

I answer the first half of the questionnaire and do some more sitting, waiting for my name to be called. All of this so far was the dress-rehearsal. Next up: the interrogation back room with another live human being.

I move to the back room, and the nurse shuts the door. They take my blood pressure, temperature (orally, you pervert) and my pulse. I have all three. Yahoo, I pass. Again, I feel like a champion. Then the hard questions start.

They ask me if I have any horrible diseases, or if I have ever taken money or drugs for sex. The first time they asked me this I was a little taken aback, but it makes sense. There are no refunds if you get someone's blood—basically they are making sure that your loved ones are getting only the high-quality stuff.

There is one weird question that I have not figured out as to why they care. They want to know if I have ever handled monkey fluids. I'm thinking that if a monkey peed on me, I would definitely remember, and I would definitely not be bragging about it. I am glad they asked—this is not information that is usually volunteered at parties. "Hey, check out Gary. He's single, available and has a PhD in Psychology. Oh, and in 1987 a monkey peed all over his neck while he was in India. He hates talking about it."

After the questions, it is show time. The nurse leads me to the big room—the one with huge, comfy chairs and needles everywhere. Enough questions. Time to pump. Some. Blood!

I take off my comfortable hoodie and show off my guns (short sleeve T-shirt). I sit in a massive, oversized sofa chair and some light rock music plays quietly in the background. I hate needles, so I just tell the nurse-lady that I am afraid of needles. They are usually pretty good about it and don't make me feel too wimpy. These people are usually pretty skilled with the needle—after all, they are poking people literally all day long. I would hope that eventually they would be relatively good at it. After Jenny the intern screws up the tenth needle of the day, the boss probably steps over the passed out patrons and tells Jenny she might want to pursue accounting or refrigeration technician school. Confused Jenny is told that she is not supposed to make the volunteer donors cry as she digs the needle around in their arm—and you have to stop digging once they fall to the floor.

There is a quick poke and then I just sit there for about six minutes. I use this time to glance around the room at the other people. I usually see people from literally all walks of life—old people, young people, different races, men, women—the blood services place doesn't care about any of that. Just make sure that a monkey hasn't peed on your neck. I know that much.

After six minutes, the little baggy is full of blood and the nurse-lady comes back to yank the needle out of the arm. I get a little rinky-dinky cotton swab and they ask me if I want a bandage or some cool pink rubber bandage tape that wraps around the arm a couple of times. I have hairy arms (at least they are hairier than a woman's arms—I hope) so I request the pink rubber bandage instead of the tape. This serves two purposes: the first is that it doesn't hurt when I unwrap the bandage a few hours later, but more importantly, the other reason is that the huge pink rubber bandage is like a neon sign flashing "THIS GUY GAVE BLOOD". I feel like a Civil War solider marching through the lunchroom, my pink rubber arm bravely hanging on as I weakly ask for free soup. And crackers. And another soda. They also have cookies. Did I mention that my arm is in a rubber pink sling? I need the cookie.

Eye Surgery Part One: I Go Blind

Since I already discussed at great length the gory, horrific details of giving blood, I might as well go all the way and talk about the eye surgery. Yes, I am one of those people who got their eyes LASIKed. My name is Karl, I am a survivor, and here is my story.

I used to have awesome eyesight. When I say "used to," I am referring to when I was about eight years old. I could watch Bugs Bunny from all the way across the living room! (Disclaimer: I am so old that I remember what it was actually like to change the television by getting up out of the chair and walking over to the TV.)

I don't know when exactly my eyesight started to fade, but it was a very gradual process. Fast forward to me in my twenties: my grandpa phoned me up and asked me if I could drive him to the airport. Because I am an awesome grandkid, I said yes. It also meant that I could drive his cool new sedan, instead of my twelve-year-old Toyota Tercel hatchback. I am proud to say that I never received a speeding ticket while driving the Tercel—not because I am great driver, but because the car couldn't exactly "go fast". Anyway, I was driving this brand-new sedan to the airport with my grandma and grandpa along for the ride.

As we were blasting up the highway to the airport, I was too busy talking to notice that there was an exit. When my grandpa pointed it out, I did what I thought was an "over the shoulder" check and then proceeded to scream across three lanes to the exit. Hey, I did an "over the shoulder" check, what more could I do? Now, we can argue all day about "who ran who" off the road, and I'm sure that the other driver (who wound up technically in the ditch) was very angry. But let's be absolutely clear: at least some of his back tire was still on the shoulder, so technically he was at least partially still on the road. He wasn't "entirely" in the ditch. Let's not be dramatic, people.

I figured I might have a vision problem after that incident, but I just chalked it up to a bad driver (the bad driver being the other guy—not me). About two months later, I was hanging out at a restaurant that happens to be at the top of a rather large building. I was about fifty stories up. It was just after sundown, so there were a bunch of other office buildings with the lights on, and of course lots of a little cars scooting around downtown far, far below.

I was hanging out with a couple of people at the party, and they were pointing out things that were happening at street level. Hey, check out that guy walking to the parkade! Wow that is a cool car. I was nodding, looking out the same window that they were. I thought they were kidding, since I couldn't clearly see any of the things that they were talking about. What do you mean, there is a guy vomiting in a garbage can? I'll have to take your word for it. What? There is an old lady being chased by two street toughs? If you say so. I thought that they were joking around and basically making stuff up about what was happening. They eventually found out that I couldn't see what was going on. One of the guys at the party took off his glasses and handed them over to me to try them on.

I put on these lenses and I was stunned. A whole world of crystal-clear events were going on! Okay, okay—admittedly, it was still the same boring stuff that was going on before—cars running through yellow lights, honking their horns at jaywalkers and dummies dropping cigarette butts on the sidewalk—but I could see the dummies! This was very exciting.

That settled that—a physical was in order. Well, more specifically, an eye exam was in order, but for some reason the doctor demanded that I take a physical. Makes sense—I need to get a pair of glasses, so please take off your pants. I was sitting on the butcher paper at the doctor's office (with no pants on) wondering if maybe I could see the large letters on the poster better if my naked bum cheeks were cold. I was in no position to judge—I was just a guy who never went to medical school and now had no pants sitting on some wax paper like corned beef at the deli. Anyway, I was awarded a clean bill of health and some poor eyesight. I needed corrective lenses (not too bad, but enough to warrant eyeglasses).

Shopping for glasses is a weird experience because there are fourteen million different frames. The prescription is set by the doctor—but literally everything else is up for grabs. Even the size of the glass in the glasses can be changed around—do you want little thin squares? Rectangles? Ovals? What about huge, round lenses that look like they should be given back to the professional snooker player that you stole them from? Did someone say monocle on a chain?

I wasn't worried too much about how I would look with glasses—I figured that I could see better with them, and if someone was making fun of me, now I could make out their facial features enough to identify them. No more laughing at me, mister fuzzy! Many of the glasses that are offered for sale are very stylish (or so I've been told—I'm a guy who wears sweatpants and a hoodie most of the time). However, there's one thing I haven't figured out. It's the person who wears the glasses with no lenses in them. Is this some sort of fashion statement? It looks kind of dumb to me. A hat—even a stylish hat—it has a purpose: protect your head from the sun or the rain. Or, possibly, to hide your head so that people don't know that you couldn't be bothered to wash your hair. Either way. I wonder sometimes if people know that they look ridiculous wearing glasses with no lenses. Good thing there are no lenses in the frames so that their face won't be too damaged when someone inevitably punches them in the nose.

I wore prescription eyeglasses for about a year. It was okay. Not great, but okay. I had trouble seeing far away. I think that made be nearsighted. That was me. Nearsighted guy. I found that the glasses were fine for day-to-day driving and walking around the office, but when I played sports it was horrible. I was playing some recreational hockey (as I'm Canadian, I'm legally obligated to skate at least once every thirty days, or the government deports you). I could still see without the glasses, but with glasses, I figured I would be good enough to actually touch the puck! So I bought some... well, I guess officially they are called "sports glasses", but they looked like big, clunky racquetball goggles. They were made of plastic, looked about three inches thick, and had a big, white elastic band keeping them on. They worked, however. I could see, I could see! Well, I could see for the first five minutes, anyway. You see, when you play sports, the human body has a tendency to sweat and heat up. So after my first shift, I would skate back to the bench and my glasses would completely and utterly fog up. I couldn't see a thing.

To make matters worse, to protect my face, I wasn't wearing a visor, but rather a full cage. So I couldn't actually touch my huge insect goggles. As long as I was moving, I was okay, but as soon as I stopped, my face instantly went "full white out" and I was watching hockey through a fog storm.

The way I picture it, I had two choices. The first was to put my stick down, take off my hockey gloves, undo my protective metal cage, wipe down the glasses, and then put the facemask back on, put on my hockey gloves and finally try to pick my stick off the floor. Great way to spend forty seconds in-between shifts. Since I don't enjoy being yelled at by my friends as to why I am undressing thirty times a game, this did not appeal to me.

The second option, and the one that I eventually went with, was to stand up and bob my head back and forth quickly. Since wind going by my goggles meant that they wouldn't fog up, I just head butted the air in front of me and tried to simulate an air current.

Of course, to anyone watching me on the bench, I looked like that little duck that people buy in the office—you know, the one who you put next to the drink of water. He bobs up and down, and looks so cute! That was me. I'm also guessing that some people just figured I was hardcore Jewish and was treating the fiberglass bench and hockey glass like my own little wailing wall.

The first game was rough, but afterwards I went out to a sports store and discovered some "anti-fogging" spray that I could spritz onto my goggles and then work into the plastic.

Sheesh, this was a lot of work. I had forked over money for the goggles, the prescription lenses, and now anti-fogging spray, which felt suspiciously like cooking oil.

Life in the office was not much better. Even just wearing my regular glasses, I was always terrified of losing or sitting on them. I finally went back to the eye store and bought a six-month supply of disposable contact lenses. I figured that this would allow me to switch up my look (like a fashion model, or someone trying to run from the law) and also see normally while not having lenses in front of me. I wound up taking about forty-five minutes to put the first pair in—I discovered that it was really, really difficult to shove foreign objects onto my eyeballs. Who knew?

The contact lenses actually worked pretty good, but they would get itchy by the end of the workday and I didn't really like the idea of having plastic sitting up against my eyeball. One day, I was sitting at my desk, and suddenly... "blip". I couldn't see out of my left eye. Everything had turned instantly fuzzy. What was up with that?

Like a hospital patient rejecting a baboon heart, my body had suddenly and dramatically rejected the contact lens. Or I had weird eyeballs. Or I didn't put them in correctly. Or a gust of wind had come by. I am much, much too lazy to hang out at "carpet level" trying to find a soiled piece of microscopically-thin plastic. It's gone. Goodbye, left contact. Luckily, I had some backup pairs handy and just shoved another one in there. I wasn't going to scour the carpet for an old, dirty contact lens, right?

Funny story: the contact lens wasn't on the floor.

It turned out it was still in my eye. It had decided to go in behind my eye. And just kind of hang out there for a while.

About two days latter, I noticed that my eye was getting really itchy and sore. I looked in the mirror and saw a little piece of plastic sticking out from under my eyeball. Hmm... that was weird. I did the logical thing and spent forty-five minutes trying to summon up the courage to touch my eyeball, get a hold of it and ultimately pull this piece of slimy, stinky plastic out of my eye socket.

As I held the greasy, folded up piece of plastic in my hand, I said no more. No more! Specifically, I said "eww... no more." I made the appointment for the eye surgery.

Eye Surgery Part Two: Under The Laser

I wouldn't say I was terrified of the eye doctor, but I was a little nervous. I went to the doctor's office for an "orientation" and a "discussion" about whether or not I was a good "candidate". Good grief—I wasn't adopting a Somalian baby, I was getting my eyes worked on.

You know it is serious stuff when they have entire evenings devoted to orientation and information. People's first reaction to getting their eyeballs hit with a laser beam is to shout, "no way!" So the response is always the same: just come to the orientation. It's just an orientation! We promise, no lasers at the orientation.

A buddy of mine had heard me complaining about the contact lenses, and then found out that I was headed off to the eye doctor's for the mysterious orientation. He knew that I was thinking of getting the eye surgery in the future and he made a point of coming over and talking with me. He told me that he had had the eye surgery done.

"But," I stated, looking closely at this face, "you are wearing glasses."

"Exactly."

"So it didn't work?"

"Well," he said, "if by 'worked' you mean that it hurt like hell and my eyes were no different, then yes it worked great!"

Uh oh. That's not what I meant at all! In fact, I had meant the exact opposite.

"Can't you go back and get the surgery done again?" I asked.

"I could," he replied, "but I would rather take a big mallet right in the nuts."

Uh oh. I wouldn't like to get hit in the nuts with a mallet, so this seemed like a scary option (both the eye surgery and the nut mallet).

But hey, it was just an orientation! No lasers at the orientation: that was their guarantee. I promised myself that if I entered the office that evening and saw even one person with a laser rifle, I was out. If Chewbacca was standing at the door, I was turning around and leaving.

I went to the orientation at the doctor's office to learn if I was a good candidate. I sat in a big room with twenty other people who were looking pretty nervous—probably as nervous as me. I thought I was hiding it, but then again, probably everyone did. If a guy in a Wookiee costume had come around the corner, about fifteen people would have started screaming and climbing over each other to get through the doorway.

The doctor's assistant came out and introduced herself. Then the lights dimmed. If Pink Floyd music was going to start, I knew it would probably be followed by a laser-light show, and I was out. They promised no lasers at the orientation! But instead, it was just a movie. We watched a ten-minute film about laser eye surgery. The film started off great—there were lots of smiling ladies and guys throwing Frisbees and hugging their dogs. So far, so good. I didn't see anyone standing around with blood pouring from their face. Although, to be fair, I knew a little bit about movies—any blood-face people would probably have been edited way down in post-production.

Then, after the film, the lights went up and the doctor himself emerged from the shadows. It was like the headliner emerging at the comedy club. Alright, enough nurse and movie, this is the guy that we paid no money yet to actually see! The doctor seemed really smart, although my only basis for this was that he was pointing at a really expensive-looking machine that apparently shot lasers. I am guessing that you must have a licence or something in order to be able to shoot laser beams—especially shooting lasers into people's faces! He also wasn't wearing any glasses and appeared to be able to look in the same general direction as where our voices were coming from, so I took that to be a good sign.

I don't know if it was the cool machine, the doctor showing off his ability to see, or the dog and human playing Frisbee together in the movie, but they had convinced me. I booked my appointment for the testing. I had another week of wearing eyeglasses (I couldn't muster the courage to stick more thin plastic into my eye socket, so the contacts were rotting in my closet).

The week passed slowly. Finally the day of the big appointment was here. This wasn't the actual surgery—the medical team had to test me first to see if I was a good "candidate". What did that mean? If I was rude or ignorant they were not going to take my money? Are there different types of people with crummy vision? I hoped that I would pass whatever testing they were going to throw at me. Maybe that was the test—when you walked in, they threw you a tennis ball. If you caught it, they screamed "liar!" and kicked you out. Made sense.

When I went back to the optometrist's office for the testing, I was happy to see that the same doctor's assistant was working there. At least she was still employed—this doctor was sounding more and more legitimate. She gave me some eye drops and I started sticking my face into various machines that looked like binoculars attached huge microscopes.

"Okay," the assistant said. "Which one is more blurry?" I was looking at two fuzzy Es. They were both fuzzy. The E on the left was fuzzy. The E on the right was fuzzy.

"Umm..." I responded. "The right?"

We did this a few times, but to be honest they all looked fuzzy. It was difficult to figure out why everything kept looking fuzzy—oh right, I wasn't wearing my glasses and I was peeking through a weird tube at some tiny letters! She kept adjusting the machine a little bit and I kept pointing out fuzzy objects— E, I, 2, B, etc. At least I think it was a B. Did I mention I had taken off my glasses and had stuck weird eye drops in my face? I couldn't see anything and I wondered what would happen if I got all of the questions wrong. Would they kick me out? Or would the doctor feel sorry for the blind guy and give me free surgery? Should I start guessing wrong on purpose in order to gain sympathy? It would be like at the movie theatre, when they offer a promotional upgrade from medium popcorn to large popcorn. Hey, I like free popcorn! What if I got more surgery because I answered the questions even more pathetically than I already was? Maybe I would wind up with even better vision than what I paid for. Maybe I would be the guy who could finally see through walls. Heat vision? Was that a real thing? I would come in handy when it was time to shovel the walkway in the winter, that much I knew.

I saw a fuzzy "Y" and had the overwhelming urge to shout out "triangle!" but I kept my composure and decided to play honestly. That free surgery upgrade, if it existed, would go to someone who truly was blind, or possibly someone who was a better liar than I was.

After about thirty minutes of me looking at little letters, we were done. They had all the data they needed to chop open my face and start shaving off pieces of eyeball.

The good news came back right away—I was a candidate for the surgery. Woo hoo! Either I was the right type of blind, or my credit application had been approved. I held my head up, knowing that I was a "good candidate". I wasn't sure if I was a good candidate because I was young enough that my eyes were able to adjust to the surgery, or because I had enough room on my credit card. Either way, I was going to go under and get my eyes zapped.

"I'm a little nervous about the procedure," I complained to the assistant. "Are you sure it doesn't hurt?"

"Well," she said, "did you feel anything during the tests?"

I was confused. I was just looking at some fuzzy letters through a microscope. "No, I didn't feel a thing."

"Do you remember those eye drops that you took?"

I nodded. She explained, "those drops numb your eyes. The lenses that you were looking through to see the letters? Those lenses were pushed up right against your eyeball."

Ewwwwwww! I wasn't so scared anymore—if I couldn't feel some microscope lens, I would be fine. Although, come to think of it, that microscope lens would have been pressed up against other eyeballs. Other gross, diseased eyeballs.

I started to get nervous again.

The actual eye surgery was great—I was in and out of the doctor's office in literally twenty minutes. I walked in, they put in some drops, I had to wait about five minutes for them to "do their thing" and I was in the chair. They didn't knock me out—I was fully conscious because you have to look at a little laser beam. I guess it doesn't work when your eyeballs are rolled up in the back of your head.

The only weird part was that once the eye drops start working, you have zero desire to blink. Eyes blink because they get dry, and if they don't feel anything, you just sit there without blinking. The doctor clamped open my eyeballs like in a horror movie and it was like watching him use a scalpel on the windshield of my car—I could see it all, but I couldn't feel a thing.

He turned on the laser beam and I stared at a little red laser for twenty seconds. Then he did the other eye and I stared for twenty seconds. Then I was done. I was home sitting in the dark an hour later.

Actually, there were two weird parts: the other weird thing was that it smelled like burning hair—like when you have the hairdryer on for a while and you smell that weird burning smell.

"That's your eyeball," he said. The doctor was wearing a surgical mask but I am pretty sure he was smiling when he said it. Eww!

It has been ten years and I can still see great. I haven't had to wear glasses or contacts or anything like that. No more picking skinny plastic pieces of goop out of my eye socket!

Self-Checkout

How did people ever buy groceries before the self-checkout machine? Well, I'm guessing in a somewhat orderly and mundane fashion—a working professional would scan your items and then a bagboy would put your items in a grocery bag. Is bagboy offensive? I don't know anymore. Nowadays, is it politically correct to use the term bagperson instead? Bag attendant? I don't think anyone cares about the terminology anymore—primarily because no one has ever put my groceries in a bag during my lifetime. The only reason I know that bagboys used to exist is from watching old black-and-white episodes on television. Hey, look! The Waltons are shopping for groceries and a stranger is trying to steal their salami! No wait, it is a bagboy. The mythical bagboy. (Or bagperson.)

There are no bagboys, baggirls or bagpeople at all at the super grocery store where I do my shopping. For legal reasons, on the advice of my lawyer and primarily from my imagination, I will not reveal the name of the super super market chain of Canadian stores. That would be wrong. They are super, however, in their prices and their selection. It is a real Canadian store, and it is super. A "super store", if you will. The only part of the deal that is not so super is the checkout.

My mom, for example, won't even go into the store. It's like post-traumatic stress or something. "Life's too short," she says, standing out front with her arms crossed. "Bagging groceries of that size and weight is a two-person job in that store. And I'm only one person." She ventures to the Co-Op or the Safeway, or someplace that actually helps you at the checkout. Sure, their prices are ridiculously high (like thirty more cents for a ten-pound block of cheese) but at least they have staff who sometimes will bag the groceries. I even saw a young man once helping an old lady out to her car! Either that, or the poor grand kid was suckered into spending "quality time" with Grandma, which meant walking around Safeway while an old lady buys lederhosen and figs.

Because I am so cheap, I go the huge super supermarket. I

figure I have two options:

1. get there right when they open, and beat the crowd
2. get there at 2:00 pm and try to pick the lineup that will get me out of there before I need to shave again

I almost always get there right when it opens. Would I like to sleep in on a Saturday morning? You bet! We all have dreams. But I am not going to spend twelve hours in a lineup watching families of seven buy eighty-pound skids of laundry detergent. It's just not going to happen. So, I drag myself out of bed, get in the car, get over to the store, and beat the rush.

Here's the part that kills me: because it is so early, there is only one checkout open. So there is a huge lineup already, even though there are only ten people in the whole store.

My quick complain letter: dear super store, if that is your real name. If I get up out of bed and actually put on pants, I would appreciate another cashier. Thank you.

I was mentally relegating myself to a lifetime of standing in lines in the early hours of the morning, but then one day something incredible happened: I walked in and saw self-checkout machines. Six of them! Robots had either been built and imported to perform boring, mundane tasks instead of cashiers, or machines from the future had arrived and were sent here to kill us. The first option seemed more plausible.

No, wait. I froze in terror, looking at these self-checkout machines. It just dawned on me.

I was the cashier now.

Hmm. I had to weight the options. Was I was okay with this? I determined that I was. I was okay with this because

1. I am not 100 years old
2. I can read at least some English

So I figured I could operate the self-checkout. For the most part, I can. I have been using the self-checkout now for many years, and with some success. In fact, I pride myself on getting to the terminal, quickly scanning and paying, and then walking by with a derisive look on my face at the poor sap who is still trying to find the bar code on his box of Cheerios. Hope you remember what your family looks like, old man! Because at your current checkout rate of speed, you won't be seeing them for a while.

The self-checkout works. It does. Honest. However, there are a few quirks in the system, so here are some ways to speed up your life and get through the self-checkout in a timely fashion.

1. Don't buy melon. I find that if you buy a cantaloupe for some reason, the machine freaks out. Suddenly I am "waiting for an attendant". Why are we calling security over here? It's a melon. Everyone calm down. It is easier to just avoid cantaloupe altogether—not for health reasons, but because I just don't have the patience to wait for the clerk to eventually come over. Is it possible to be racist against fruit? The machine loves bananas. But melon just makes it angry. It's like "stop and frisk" for certain types of produce. It's not right, but it's not a fight that I want to have with the machine at this point in time.

2. Don't sit on the scale. This primarily applies to annoying little children who think it is totally awesome to sit on the part of the machine where you put your food after you have scanned it. It is a scale. Get off and get out. What are you doing in the store anyway? Your mommy shops here? Go wait in the car! There should be a thirty-dollar minimum to even get in the store. I don't care that it is 8:00 am on a Saturday. It should be like a nightclub—big, burly bouncers are standing at the front door, turning away little poor kids. "No, my mom is in there," they would complain. Beat it kid, show me the Benjamins if you want to get in the VIP area with the melons and the bananas.

3. Don't have more than 300 items. Now, I know that the sign says a maximum of 25 items, but it has been my opinion that everyone ignores this sign. No one except me has less than 25 items. One person I saw was using the self-checkout with two shopping carts! Dude, go stand in the regular line unless your last name is actually Superstore. If that is the case, then go for it, since your dad probably owns the place.

4. Don't buy produce of any kind. Forget the melon. The melon is out. Most of the time, it has no problem with bananas. But hear me out. This advice also extends to celery, apples, pears, and whatever that weird turnip-thing is over in the roots section that isn't a turnip. I've never seen anyone buy it. I am wondering if they just start digging up tree roots outside and bringing them into the produce section, wondering if they can make some extra money. "Hey George, grab a shovel. Someone bought a stinky tree root yesterday—yeah, the one that we dug up for fun—it's gone! We need to replenish."

The reason I hate the produce is that you have to weigh it, and that takes time. Plus, there is no bar code. So you have suddenly become a student at DeVry. Now you are a computer programmer, navigating through menus, pictures of beets and romaine lettuce and cucumbers in order to find your seedless African grapes. It's not worth it! A bag of Cheez Puffs are 99 cents and they have a bar code. Scan it and get the hell out of there.

Baby Pictures

Do you have kids? If so, you probably have pictures of them up in the house. Especially if they are little kids. I was recently over at a buddy's place and noticed that he had pictures of his children up on every wall. These were professionally-done photos—like at the department store, you drag your kids in there and the pose for pictures and then you have photographic evidence that your reproduced.

If the kids are small, you can dress them up in literally any outfit and they look fine. My buddy had a picture of one of kids on the wall, and the small child was wearing a cowboy hat, little mini chaps and that was about it. He was a three-year-old cowboy! Adorable!

You can't get away with that when you're thirty. You don't see a full-grown man with no shirt on and a cowboy hat sitting in front of a fake forest. Grandma is showing off the picture to her bridge club. "That's Mike, he's my youngest... he's thirty-two. He's a sheriff at the Wal-Mart photo place!"

Little kids not only can wear anything they want in the photos without it looking weird, but they can do anything as well and it's all good. There are literally no rules. If you have a bowl of spaghetti? Dump it on the two-year-old kid's head. He loves it, the parents love it, and no one seems to find this strange. "Here's our picture of little Kenny, we poured cereal and milk all over him and then a stranger took his picture." Adorable!

The little costumes are a bit strange to me. No four-year-old kid is a real police officer. You don't need to put the hat and sunglasses on mini-constable toddler. You aren't fooling anyone. "I don't see an ID badge, but the kid on the tricycle is a police officer, I swear. I've seen a photo where he's wearing sunglasses and holding the tiniest, cutest pistol you've ever seen. But then again, I remember seeing him covered in pasta as well—maybe he was working undercover."

All-Inclusive Resorts

I just got back from a great vacation in Jamaica. We're talking sand, surf, sun, and, of course, boatloads of food and gallons upon gallons of alcohol.

I'm not sure I understand why there is the all-inclusive resort. I mean, don't get me wrong—I love them—you get off the airplane, put your wallet and your passport in the safe in your room and forget about them (and everything else) for a week. I just think that having a mile of perfect beach, scorching sun and breezy tropical winds should be enough to entice pasty bloated tourists like me each year to leave the frozen wasteland that I call home.

"Hmm, there seems to be an island in the middle of the Caribbean. Let me look it up on the computer. Beautiful weather... lots of sand and beach... I'm still on the fence. If they have more than twelve pies, I will consider leaving immediately."

The first and most wonderful thing that you have going for you at the all-inclusive resort is the free food and booze. I happen to be a skinny guy but, gun to my head, I can pack it away. People have witnessed my show at the Chinese Buffet and they brag about it. At least that's what I am telling myself they are doing as they recount the story to strangers and point in my direction. Anyway, what is great about the food at the resort is that you can stack your plate up high with all sorts of exotic meats, ice cream, pie, pizza, more ice cream, fish, fruit, things you think might be fruit, and bacon. I've come to realize that wherever you are from in this world, if you are visiting a resort, you will place some sort of salty meat on the top of your plate. I don't care if there is ice cream under there. The bacon is going on the top.

Hey, if you don't like it, then don't eat it! You aren't paying any more for a huge plate of waste than if you are trying to be responsible. Don't worry about making the waiter upset. They love cleaning up your four half-eaten plates of papaya and pineapple. You weren't sure if you would like the chocolate cake, so you only took three pieces. They get it—the resort crowd is not the responsible crowd. If they were, someone would eventually get out of the pool bar to use the bathroom. I have yet to witness that. Eight straight hours of drinking Pina Colodas and no one ever gets out of the pool. I can do the math.

You see all sorts of interesting people at the all-inclusive resort. I happen to fall under the "happy drunk guy who still thinks he is ten years younger than he is" category. I'm in the pool trying to play water volleyball against 19-year-old college students from Omaha. I am not a professional volleyball player. So I totally understand why I am terrible. But here's my question: they don't even have water in Nebraska—at least I don't think they do. So why are there Omaha dudes with cut abs spiking a ball into my face? Oh well, it's been ninety minutes since my meal in between lunch and dinner—I think I'll grab a snack instead.

Everything becomes a big deal on vacation. Have you ever had a drink at your house? Maybe you get home from a long day, and you are watching television, and you kind of walk over to the cabinet and pour yourself a drink? No one applauds, do they? For some reason, if you order a couple of drinks at 10:02 a.m., strangers are applauding and pointing. Maybe they are doctors, or they happen to own shares in a rum plantation. In any event, they are cheering you on. Destroy that liver, ASAP!

The huge competitive tanners come out of the wordwork on these tropical vacations. The minute people are at the resort, the shirt is off. Boom. Guys are topless within seconds. Women run like Florence Griffith-Joyner to their hotel room and spin around like Wonder Woman three times before dashing off to the beach. It might take her four days to pack for the vacation, but within forty-five seconds she is on the beach, in a chair, facing the sun like a photo-sensitive Venus Flytrap. We also need the US Magazine and the largest sunglasses that a human cranium can safely support. It's like two Buzz Aldrin astronaut shields and some wire rims. Hey, I say good for you—it's all anyone ever asks about after you get back from holidays anyway.

Co-worker: Where were you?

Me: I was in Jamaica.

Co-worker: Where's the tan?

Me: I don't want to get cancer.

Co-worker: I don't see much of a tan.

Me: I had a pretty good time.

Co-worker: So... no tan?

By the way—how come at home I can make my bathroom towel last a month before it finally marches itself to the washing machine, and yet on vacation I am going through eight towels in one day? They have a little hotel resort sign on the counter that says "save the environment, only put towels in the tub that you don't want to use again." Well, guess what. Every single towel is going in that tub. I'm breaking into neighbour's hotel rooms, taking their towels, and throwing them in the tub. The thought of even looking at a towel more than once becomes instantly disgusting. I'm wearing the same T-shirt four days in a row, but I'm going through towels like toilet paper.

Anyway, Jamaica is great if you like sun and nine meals a day.

Spring Has Sprung: Put Some Clothes On

Living in Canada, there is a tradition up here that happens every spring. "Spring" is defined as when the temperature gets above freezing for more than twelve consecutive hours. If you see a puddle of water outside of someone's home, chances are very high that it is now officially spring, at least in the minds of us Canadians.

Whenever spring is, the tradition that I'm speaking of is the Canadian custom of taking off clothing as soon as it stops snowing. I was out driving around town yesterday and I saw shorts. Keep in mind, it was about eight degrees Celsius out. You still don't need a refrigerator at this point—just find some shade by an evergreen tree and put your milk over there for a few days and it would be fine. There is some unwritten rule that says that if you can bare some legs and the blood technically continues to flow to your extremities, then you owe it to yourself—and society—to walk around in your shorts, a bathing suit, or even just some underwear on your way to the grocery store. The logic seems to be that if you are not wearing a winter jacket, apparently pants are now optional as well.

My neighbourhood still has large patches of snow around, although there is some sad, brown goopy grass pockets poking its stubby blades through in some yards. This means that it is time to rake the lawn! One neighbour is literally raking the grass around the clumps of snow. Is this really helping? How bored are you inside the home that you see one blade of grass and now we are working in the yard? Isn't this nature's way of telling you to go inside and watch Wheel of Fortune? It always seems to be the seniors who are doing this—I'm forty years old, and I can barely muster the energy to glance out the window. Meanwhile, there's an eighty-five year old lady raking her front yard like a cat in the litter box. Scrape, scrape, scrape—well, I think all of the brown goop (leaves) has been separated from the other brown goop (grass).

If I ever lived on a farm, I think that the rooster would

eventually get on my nerves. However, the rooster is doing its job—the sun comes up and this animal is screaming at the top of its lungs. Okay, I get that. We have a similar situation in the big city. I call him "motorcycle guy". He's the cock of the town. When spring has sprung, it is now apparently time to rev the motorcycle in the garage. Mind you, the bike is not actually making an appearance at this point—it is like the space shuttle. The bike needs about four hours of preparation time in the garage first before finally "launching" at two miles per hour onto the mud-puddled, still half-frozen street. Hey, is that Buzz Aldrin on a motorbike? I sure hope so—that would be about the only situation where I would be okay with four hours of revving a motorcycle in a garage. (Because then I would have an astronaut as a neighbour, and I would put the mail that was addressed to me in his mail box so he would be forced to come over to my house to drop off the mail and then I would invite him in and spend the next three days demanding to know if the moon missions were faked. Or we could just watch Seinfeld reruns.)

The thing I don't get about motorcycles is that they don't really do anything. Even a tiny car can carry things—like groceries or supplies—from point A to point B. But a motorcycle just carries the driver and maybe, sometimes, in rare instances, someone else. There seems to be ninety minutes of preparation time, which involves a leather scuba outfit, cowboy boots, and often a helmet with the spike on top. The spike? Really? Okay, Kaiser. Let me stop you right there. You can tell that the government in this case is making the motorcycle guy wear the helmet and he doesn't want to. Motorcycle guy is like "alright, I will comply with your laws. I will wear the helmet. However, I will affix a huge spike on the top of the helmet, so that in the event of a crash, I will become a human javelin. I may be safe, but if I stab enough people, there will be a new law passed that says all pedestrians must wear Kevlar body armour when walking down the street."

So now, thanks to the Kaiser (that's what a lot of us are calling him after the accident where he impaled himself on three people walking to the mall), we all have to wear Kevlar vests. Cover up, people! Except for the legs of course—it is technically spring, after all.

Boring Road Trips

I travel a little bit for my job, and this means a few hours in a car, driving from town to town. One of the big problems that I have, and I'm sure that you do as well, is staying alert on the road. After all, driving along a highway in a comfortable car can be tough—you have air conditioning or heat, plush seats, and (if the windows are rolled up) it is quiet and calm.

I never had this problem when I was younger. I had a little hatchback that I drove around for a while when I was in university. First of all, you will never fall asleep at the wheel if your car does not have power steering. It's impossible. And speaking of impossible—the other thing that is impossible is to actually turn the vehicle. The first time I drove the hatchback, I was literally pulling out of the parking stall and getting ready to test drive it. I wanted to turn right. I thought about turning right, my arms tried to turn the wheel clockwise. I had dreams, people. Goals. And the car just kept going straight. The car decided that I needed to do more push ups, or maybe start injecting steroids into my bum. I'm not sure. Luckily I slammed on the brakes and the car screeched to a halt (well, more like the car slowed down and eventually stopped) and I declared the car "undrivable!". Power steering is a huge advancement in technology—for those of us who don't do "weights" it is like the printing press or penicillin.

One of the nice features of that old car was that the glove box had fallen off. I'm not sure where it went, but it wasn't with the car. Somebody, somewhere, had a glove box just hanging out in their garage. They probably had one extra pair of gloves that was just driving them crazy. Rip out the glove box and sell the car. Problem solved. However, for me, the guy now driving this hatchback with no glove box, that meant that for the passenger, there was a piece of cardboard where the glove box should be, and the passenger would get icy winter air blowing right on their genitals. The constant complaining keeps the driver alert in the winter.

Anyway: you are out on the boring highway and you are in your comfortable, swanky, high-class car that has all the glass in the windows and the heater even works. You snob! Well, the joke is on you. You are so comfortable that you will eventually fall asleep at the wheel and veer off the highway. Actually, that is not really a joke, but you get the point. We don't want that. So here are a few tips to stay awake, alert and have some fun while driving to your destination.

1. Take off your shirt. Now hold on ladies, hear me out. Of course, I am advocating this for the dudes only. Unless, of course, ladies you are into that sort of thing. In which case, try it out for a couple of months and see how it feels. But if you are offended, then of course I am talking to the guys only here.

First of all guys, you are going to notice your nipples quite a bit. Keep your eyes on the road. Trust that nothing in the car is going to bite or attack your nipples. The air rushing around the car, and the concerned looks of other drivers will keep you alert and refreshed!

2. Sing to the radio. What I am talking about here is not just "humming" along. I don't mean regular singing. I am talking full-blown Pavarotti. Get into it. Own the song. If you enjoy ballads, then you should have tears streaming down your face as you pull into the hotel parking lot. Making the devil sign for those heavy metal guys are okay, but just don't head bang during turns off ramps.

3. Get angry. I have turned into my father. I listen to talk radio now. Sometimes listening to a conversation can be fun, but often the topic on the radio show is kind of boring. The environment? Please. European debt crisis? Snooze. Hockey interview? That is fine—if you want to drive your car off the road! Instead, consider not only answering the questions yourself, but getting really angry while you are doing it. Example: the host of the radio program is interviewing a financial representative about retirement. The host asks about RRSPs. Now forget what the guest is going to say—you don't care. Get angry! Start ranting about how inappropriate that question is. Why is he giving you, the financial expert, the third degree about finances? How dare he! Who does he think he is! In this day and age, if someone sees you ranting and raving in the car all by yourself, they just tell themselves that you own a Bluetooth. Or maybe you have an imaginary friend, or someone very short sitting in the seat next to you. Wow, that guy is so important that he yelling at someone on the phone! Or a small child. He is a winner! Hopefully they won't be too judgemental.

Remember, if you get pulled over by the police: put your shirt on, turn down the radio, stop shouting and singing, and have some fun! Try not to get zapped with the Taser—although if you do, that would really wake you up.

Biographies

If you are ever talking to someone who is super old, but you aren't sure if they are super old, just ask them if they enjoy reading. If they say "no, I only enjoy biographies," then chances are very good that they are at least sixty years old. If they reply that they only enjoy biographies about war generals, then they are at least ninety. (And thank you for your service!)

I enjoy reading the occasional biography. There are basically two types: biographies about really good people, and biographies about really bad people.

Examples of good people:
• business leaders / CEOs
• inventors
• doctors
• sports athletes (preferably really successful ones who then have a substance-abuse or drinking problem)
• rock stars (preferably really successful ones who then have a substance abuse problem—which is pretty much every single one of them)
• military leaders

We read these biographies because we want to know what it is like to shoot the winning basket, make a ton of money, or sleep with the supermodel.

Examples of bad people:
• murderers
• multiple-murderers
• some guy who kills A LOT of people
• sports athletes—who kill people
• military leaders (if their side lost the war)

Here is my major complaint about biographies: they are very formulaic. You can pretty much just grab a biography template and fill in the blanks.

Every biography opens with the exciting part that we actually want to read about. The sports guy is sitting in the parking lot thinking about driving his car off a cliff, or the rock star is in the hospital on life support and the doctor is screaming for a needle—a needle containing life saving drugs? What a twist! And we are only on page two!

Then, unfortunately, the next part is the really boring sixty pages of the book where we jump back in time and start with the potato famine of the 17th century or some European plague. Amidst all of this medieval-time boring stuff, a great-grandfather emerges. Then we have to sit through the great-grandfather courting the great-grandmother. Did you know that Hans Blichtenzing sat outside the Belgium cheese factory all summer in 1856 in order to ask Mary Ann Vleoptara for her hand in marriage? We don't care! We are begging the author at this point—please fast forward two centuries to get to the guitar player who is shooting heroin already.

The best biographies are the "unauthorized" biographies. This is because it speaks to the real reason that we are reading the book in the first place—we want some dirt! Autobiographies can be super boring, because they are written (or dictated) by the person who lived the life. The person writing the book isn't going to admit to the uncool things that they have done in the past. Sure, they will admit to shooting the drugs, bopping the girls and making the money, but they aren't going to readily admit to one thing— being a big dummy. They won't complain about some accountant ripping them off, or worse, being lazy. They will only do this if it makes them look cool. Example of uncool lazy: Hans took the summer off to eat cake instead of bodybuilding, and as a result, he lost the big Mr. Wonderful championship. Yeah... not going to happen. Instead, it is written that Hans was screwed over because of corrupt judges. Poor Hans! Example of cool laziness: rock star is too lazy to write a new album—because of all the naked ladies running around his mansion! That lazy bum. We can't stay mad at lazy guy. He's only human, and he's a great guy! At least according to his autobiography.

Getting Engaged: The Real Story

Girls love hearing the engagement story, so dudes, you had better make it a good one. We were on vacation in Paris and I decided that it was time to ask my girlfriend Stacey to marry me. This was it. I went out and bought the ring, and then the games began.

First of all, I wondered, where am I supposed to hide a diamond ring? We were in Europe for two weeks. Yikes. The obvious answer is in the suitcase, except that I pack like a junior high school student's locker. I just take clothes and kind of stuff them in. There's no folding, there's no organization. I would never find the ring again. So here was my big plan: I stuffed the ring in the bottom of a pair of shoes that I was bringing along, and then put a sock in the shoe. Brilliant. Just to make it not look suspicious, I stuffed another sock in the other shoe. I told myself this looked normal, even though no one in the history of mankind has ever stuffed socks in shoes so neatly when they travel.

Who's looking in my suitcase you may ask? Here's my other foible: I don't really "do" laundry. I put a pair of Lulu Lemon pants in a dryer once a couple of years ago and I was pulled from the game. They weren't my pants. I didn't know. Apparently Lulu Lemon pants cost a fortune because they are the greatest fabric in the world—they can withstand sweating, stretching, exercise, et cetera—but if you put them in the dryer they are destroyed. So the coach pulled Wiebe from the game and now I am holding the clipboard on the sidelines when it comes to laundry. Don't get me wrong—I am not complaining. I can supervise the washing and the drying of the clothes and watch football at the same time. If the dryer catches fire, I will grab a fire extinguisher during the commercial. That is the extent of me doing laundry. So Stacey has "all access" to the suitcase since I will just put stinky underwear right back in the suitcase. It's not an issue (for me, anyway) because I can tell, most of the time, which clothes I have worn before.

So the suitcase has shoes in there, and the shoes have socks in there, and there is a ring hidden in there somewhere. We wound up in Paris, France. My big idea was to propose at the Eiffel Tower. This was the plan. If you haven't been to the Eiffel Tower, then you are probably thinking "wow, that is the greatest". If you have been to the Eiffel Tower, then you know that this is a terrible idea. I will explain now the difference between the marketing of Paris and the reality of Paris.

The marketing: you show up at the Eiffel Tower via a horse carriage. Everything smells like lavender. You put away your parasol and ascend the beautiful Eiffel Tower to the viewing platform. Some dude with a pencil moustache appears at the top with an accordion. You gaze out over the river and the Arc de Triomphe and suddenly you whip out the ring. The girl starts crying, she screams yes and you kiss on top of the world.

Enter reality.

First of all, there are gangs of gypsies roaming around the Eiffel Tower. This is what we were told upon arrival. Watch out for the gypsies. Gypsies! They are everywhere! What would have been helpful is if someone had explained to me what a gypsy looks like. I was picturing Little Steven from the E Street Band, but that was just an old guy with a bandana. Then I thought of some guy with a turban and some pointy slippers, but I am pretty sure that was a genie. So I decided that logically, with the absence of any more information, that I should be terrified of everyone. I walked into the horribly long lineup to the Eiffel Tower with my hands in my pockets, guarding the ring, my wallet and my fingers. Nice try gypsies—you aren't taking anything!

There are actually two lineups to the Eiffel Tower. Line up #1 is for VIPs like us who bought advance tickets. This meant that we were in a small lineup. Then there were all the schmoes who just showed up. They were in a way longer line. So we were feeling like big shots until we got near the front of our line.

The lines merged right at the elevator. So this meant that if you were pushy enough, you could just get into this "mosh pit" of people who were trying to get on this elevator. We did all the work in advance, researching and buying a ticket online, and then printing it off and carrying it with us halfway across the world. And we were competing with pushy we-just-thought-we-would-show-up person. Annoying.

There are four corners at the Eiffel Tower. Only one lift was operating. So that meant that you had one tiny, rickety elevator that was built in the 19th century to haul a bunch of pushy, angry and impatient tourists to the top. The doors opened, the empty elevator awaited and we as a big group pushed forward. I expected to hear Pearl Jam's Even Flow blare out of the loudspeakers. It was a mosh pit. I am pretty sure that I crushed a Spanish lady's foot—and I didn't show any remorse. Gypsies can probably smell fear and weakness anyway. I stand by my decision and I'm sure she will heal someday.

We made it onto the elevator—I was pushed up into the corner of the small metal cage, my hands stuck firm inside my pockets. No one could move. I was hoping that Stacey was on the elevator. If she wasn't, she did her best and she would be missed.

When the elevator reached the top and the doors finally burst open, people scrambled off with the same ferocity as when we got on. Being Canadian, I have been conditioned to act with at least a tiny amount of manners, so that meant that me and my girlfriend were the last ones off the elevator. The absolute last ones. Pushy Romanians first, guy with the forty pounds of camera equipment next, and then everyone else, and then us. We caught our breath and stepped out onto the observation deck.

The winds were horrible that day, my friend. You know it is bad when you use "winds". As in plural. Wind is normal—hey, we are golfing today, watch out for that wind! "Winds" means that people and property are being blown away. The winds on the top of the tower were fierce. I whipped out my little iPod to take a picture and it almost blew away. Almost iGone. We look like we are smiling in the pictures, but we are gritting our teeth and trying to remain on the concrete.

"MIND THE PICKPOCKETS" blared over the loudspeaker every ten seconds. It's hard to propose when you are hearing this over and over again. We were constantly frisking ourselves, making sure that phones, cameras and money were still in our pockets.

Me: I think that you are very special—

Tower: MIND THE PICKPOCKETS

Me: I would be honoured if you—

Tower: PICK POCKETS ARE IN THE AREA

Me: Umm...

Tower: BEWARE OF YOUR BELONGINGS

This went on for a few minutes, and I eventually abandoned the plan. The observation deck was out. Instead, Stacey said that she wanted a glass of champagne. They have one guy, in one booth, at the very top of the Eiffel Tower and all he sells is champagne. Awesome. So we buy a glass of champagne and we hand the guy a 20-Euro note.

He tells us that he has no change.

Really. You are working at literally the most famous building in the world, at the top, and you only sell one item. He seemed surprised that anyone was actually buying anything. I imagined that he phoned down to his supervisor on the ground floor. "Hey boss, you are not going to believe this. Yeah, we finally sold a glass of champagne. I know! I know! That's what I thought. Who buys this stuff? Anyway, we have no change. I never thought to bring any up when I started my shift. Yeah, bad planning on my part. But, in my defense, I didn't think that any tourist would travel all the way to Paris for champagne!"

We enjoyed the view and finally stuffed ourselves back in the squeaky elevator and made it back to solid ground. That was okay, I said to myself. I was going to propose on the lawn in front of the Eiffel Tower. Just as romantic. It's still on the property. Still counts.

So we went to the supermarket and bought some picnic stuff— some long skinny bread, some wine, and some fruit. Perfect! We picked out a spot on the lawn and ate our bread and enjoyed the majesty of the Eiffel Tower. How romantic!

Then we saw the gypsies. These creepy-looking young guys were wandering around asking people to sign some document or petition. But they were laying the paper down on tourists' purses and belongings and trying to do the old "steal your possession" trick. Get out of here, gypsies! I'm on to you guys. For the record, they were wearing regular shoes—no pointy shoes, just regular sneakers.

So they finally moved on to some other, unsuspecting tourists and we went back to eating. With eyes darting around on the hunt for creepy gypsies, or genies, who human rights advocates who wanted me sign a petition, we began eating grapes and drinking Cherry Coke.

I reached into my pocket to pull out the ring, and it was just then that three girls from Japan emerged from nowhere and set up shop six feet away from us. They decided to spend the next twenty minutes jumping up and down and taking pictures. And I mean literally jumping up and down. Like jumping jacks. I don't know what kind of cheerleading they have in Tokyo but these girls had some energy. There was the "pointing to the top of the tower", the "chest bump", the "standing on each other's shoulders"—they must have taken 300 pictures. There was selfies, twofies, and a threefie in there at some point. Anyway, the park was out. Forget the park. It wasn't going to happen. We finished the lunch and Stacey declared that she was ready to go home.

Think, man, think! If it didn't happen at the Eiffel Tower, where else could I propose? The French Army Museum? There was an Apple Store at the Louvre—in my defense, I had about ten seconds to run through different places. I loudly declared that it was time to go for a walk around the park first. I made up some story about memories, and we should smell the flowers—if she wasn't suspecting something before, she would very soon. I haven't voluntarily smelled a flower in my life and I wasn't about to start. Maybe she thought I was growing as a person? Unlikely. I had better make this happen.

We quickly got on a paved pathway and I proposed in the shadow of the Eiffel Tower. It was private, romantic and wonderful.

I guess even great wine takes some grape stomping. So despite some weird grapes, we stomped on them and created a great memory.

Consequences for Actions: All-Inclusive Resort Edition!

People love justice. There's a scene in the popular TV series Breaking Bad where the main hero Walter White gets even with a rude loudmouth at a gas station by sticking a squeegee under the hood of the loudmouth guy's expensive car, and moments later the car bursts into flames. We cheer! Yay, the jerk got three thousand dollars' worth of damage to his car. But what happens when this sort of thing occurs in real life?

Disclaimer before we begin... I didn't wreck anyone's car.

Speaking of rude loudmouths: all-inclusive resorts. I love them and I hate them. I was in Mexico this year on an awesome, all-inclusive pig fest that included six meals a day, unlimited booze with poolside service, and an employee who is probably not a licensed physician who carted around a tequila shot cart and gave ladies by the pool mysterious liquid that made people gag and cry. Typical family fun in Mexico.

Once the sun goes down, the party really gets wild. Because I am getting old, my wild partying consists of sitting in a comfortable lounge chair sipping rum punches and complaining about the extra three pounds of steak that I shouldn't have eaten. However, on our next-to-last night at the resort, things got a little weird at the evening sports bar.

Here's the scene: me and my fiancée are sitting at the bar. (She was my girlfriend at the start of the book and my fiancée near the end of the book. See, this book has the power to change lives, people!) There is an older lady sitting at the end of the bar, minding her own business, probably trying to have a good vacation, and then enters the guy. The guy is about 6' 2" and in decent shape. He looks like a young Mr. Spock, if say, Spock had drank some Martian rum or Jupiter Elixir or whatever the hell Star Trek aliens drink. Anyway, this guy had his arm draped over the older lady and the older lady didn't look very happy about it.

What to do, what to do? For me, the answer is simple: I did the "Ghandi"—meaning, for me, that I sat quietly and chugged my rum. That was my non-violent protest. Please, hold your

166

applause. My fiancée, being a woman, felt inside her brain what is known as "sympathy" and gestured for the older-lady-stranger to leave the hungry-eyed drunk guy and make her way over to where we were sitting. She was waving, come on over to the sane side of the bar!

It turns out that older lady didn't know drunk guy. She didn't like drunk guy. She wanted nothing to do with drunk guy. Her husband was a little under the weather and he was back in the hotel room, sleeping. And so older lady wanted to come downstairs for a drink. Come on, drunk guy! Personal space please! Anyway, we thought that was the end of it. Lady rescued.

Wrong.

Drunk guy shows up again, having successfully negotiated the twenty-five feet of bar stools and bright 40-watt lights of the Mexican sports bar. Hello ladies! Drunk guy shows up, wraps his arms around this older lady and exclaims that he was "interested".

"Hey," my fiancée spoke up. "That's my mom! We're here for a family reunion!" I nodded, much like Nelson Mandela would have silently nodded when he was sentenced to jail for eighteen years. Are we both heroes? Let's let history decide.

Drunk guy was from Saskatchewan and he claimed that we was interested in the older lady. Why he felt the need to mention that he was from Saskatchewan remains a mystery. Anyway, we explained that "mom" already had a "dad" and that "dad" might appear at any moment. Watch out, Saskatchewan! Saskatchewan, who was about twenty-five years old, loudly exclaimed that he was ready to be our new daddy. Really? He was implying that he wanted to beat up my father and then would buy the older lady a drink. Ladies be talkin', and a conversation between Saskatchewan and my fiancée wound up with Saskatchewan bunching up a napkin and throwing it in her face.

Wrong.

So what do we do at this point? Ghandi might have gotten up off the bar stool and started punching, but I didn't. Maybe that makes me even more Ghandi-ish. (Where's my Nobel Prize? It just seems to be all about who you know.) We told Saskatchewan to give us some personal space and thought that was the end of it. Saskatchewan noticed two guys sitting at the end of the bar—they looked about thirty, maybe thirty-five years old and were quietly sipping beers. "What are you guys looking at?" Saskatchewan yelled at them. Oh dear.

We pulled the two guys into this by exclaiming that these were our brothers. They said they were from Michigan... of course! Our brothers from Michigan. This was a family reunion! We tried to make small talk for a few minutes, but with Saskatchewan hanging out and loudly yelling "Roughriders!" at random intervals, it was not likely that any of the world's problems were going to get solved. For those reading this book who may not be from Saskatchewan, the Roughriders are the local professional football team. That still doesn't explain things, but I'm trying here.

Saskatchewan suddenly yelled that it was time to do shots. He was buying us all shots. Wow, thanks! At an all-inclusive resort? You are a hero my friend. He whipped out two 500-peso notes and threw them down at the bartender. We all froze. I did a double-take and the Michigan guy who was closest to me saw me glancing at the notes, and then at him. Michigan guy said "nope," meaning, don't say a word. Things were getting good now. Normally people tip anywhere from ten to twenty pesos for the whole evening. Saskatchewan had just dropped about $75.00 US on the table.

The bartender scooped it up like David Blaine pocketing my watch on a street corner. In one fluid motion, the bartender set up four shots on the bar—these had some sort of nasty tequila stuck in a shot glass, upside down, inside of a full, tall glass of dark brown beer. Gun to my head, I would rather have drank my own pee at this point than whatever was in that glass.

A long, drawn-out discussion ensued about who was going to drink what. There was a lot of slurring from a certain someone from Saskatchewan. Finally, we were all able to convince Saskatchewan that he had paid for the shots, and we didn't want to rob him of the chance to prove that he was "the man". Was he the man? We were starting to have our doubts. He grabbed one and downed it within ten seconds.

Wrong. (Medically speaking, that is.)

He grabbed another one and it took him about twenty seconds. I figured that would be the end of it—his heart would stop and he would be carried away by the nearby grounds crew. The guy cutting the hedges would eventually grab the broom and just sweep him out the front door. However, they breed them tough in Saskatchewan and he kept going. He downed the third. He then, unbelievably, he chugged the fourth shot with the beer. I couldn't believe what I was seeing. Remember, this guy was already completely drunk.

Saskatchewan went to put the last glass back on the bar, and he slipped on an invisible banana peel and disappeared. We heard a "sack of potatoes" thunk on the marble floor and figured that was it—time for the staff at the resort to finally dig a hole and bury this guy out in the desert. It's was nature's way. No one moved—we just enjoyed the silence for a couple of seconds. I heard Howard Cosell's voice in my head yelling "Saskatchewan is down! Saskatchewan is down!" It had been a great run, champ.

Two arms suddenly punched the air above the bar and Saskatchewan leapt up from the cold, marble floor with such ferocity that it rivalled a horror movie. Jason with the hockey mask is dead? No. No, Jason cannot die. Jason is from Saskatchewan.

We started applauding (why, exactly, we are still unsure) and suddenly Saskatchewan was taking bows and waving at the crowd. He turned to an old man who was sitting in the corner. The old man had a white beard and a smart checkered shirt—he reminded me of what Ernest Hemingway looked like if Hemingway wanted to hang out with an idiot for the evening.

Hemingway's eyes went big when he discovered that Saskatchewan was slowly walking in his direction. At this point, the eight drinks in two minutes was starting to kick in. Saskatchewan's eyes were huge and black, like a cat who spotted a squirrel through the window. Was Saskatchewan going to play with Hemingway like a mouse? Was he going to just vomit on Hemingway? "Back! BACK!" Was all that Hemingway could muster, holding out his hand like a pitch-forked villager against Frankenstein's monster.

This happened with a few other patrons at the bar—basically Saskatchewan Frankenstein would approach them, arms outstretched, eyes wide open with the thousand-yard stare—and people would recoil in horror and either politely or firmly yell at him to "get away, get away!"

What happened next is still fuzzy—not so much the details, but why they occurred. At some point during this whole "drunk zombie" march, Saskatchewan decided that the best thing to do would be to just take off his pants. So he stumbled to the middle of the bar area, and with about eighty onlookers he proceeded to undo his belt and shimmy his pants down around his ankles. I think that during the whole zombie-marching phase, people were beginning to get bored, because I pointed and shouted "look!" and people seemed genuinely surprised to be viewing white underwear.

I think we all know where this is going now.

The underwear came down.

Showing the dexterity of a hypothermic stripper, he awkwardly pulled down his underwear, exposing the hairiest bum I have ever seen. And I've seen Star Wars. This was like Chewbacca before going to the barber. I once saw a sign next to a beauty salon that said "Bikini Wax... $40.00 and up". I think this guy would have qualified for the "and up". It was both hideous and glorious—one person's bold stance against the establishment, a rallying cry for those of us who have, at one time or another, said "I simply want to be naked, and you eighty or ninety strangers are just going to have to deal with it". I was impressed.

I wish with all my heart that this was the end. I really do. But there is a little "DVD extra" that occurred: before security showed up, Saskatchewan, with his pants off and his underwear firmly entrenched between his legs, began shuffling to the bar in an effort to climb up onto the flat surface. You know... where the bartender prepares drinks? As he was naked and flailing, I wondered why do people go to Las Vegas at all? Why spend good money to the "Thunder From Down Under" when you have Chewy up on the bar, his prairie flapjack spinning in the cool Mexico night?

He got about three-quarters of the way up the bar—just far enough up that his hairy bum got dangerously close to a lady's face and about three people's martinis. Then security showed up and escorted him out.

After that, the bar kind of just petered out. People still drank their drink, and made small talk, but it wasn't the same. There was something missing. Something loud and hairy was definitely missing.

Quick epilogue: I saw Saskatchewan the next day. The sun was out, it was scorching hot, and he was in front of the towel shack, drink in hand, casually discussing Canadian football with another dude. They were casually making their way to the pool. He was totally fine. He lived. As far as the rest of us: I'm sure that we will all be fine as well—they have books and websites about post-traumatic stress disorder so we'll all figure it out.

Airports

Being tired is the worst.

Well, actually being dead is probably the worst. Because of the whole "not being around" thing. However, being tired is still pretty lousy.

I am writing this from Calgary International Airport, where I have arrived two hours before my flight. They close the check-in counter two hours before the flight, so the fear of god is drummed into passengers on travel day. I arrived at 3:45 am for a 5:45 am flight. 3:45 am. The check-in counter was open, and it took ten minutes for us to get through. We trudged over to the security line, where it took us five minutes to get through.

So now it is 4:55 am, and I have come to the sad realization that sleep at the gate is impossible. I see people lying on the floor, trying to sleep. Trying is the operative word in this case. It is, after all, a working airport. This means that announcements about dummies losing their passports in the washroom are coming over the wire every few minutes. I'm also convinced that the airport authority hires two-year-old children to run around the D wing and act like maniacs. I wonder how much it pays. There is no way that a kid is acting that annoying on their own—there has to be money involved.

There are also the wanderers. These people are bored, but they are so jacked up on coffee that they cannot fall asleep. So, instead, they wander around, large venti Frappuccino in hand, commenting on everything that they see. Hey, there's a window! There's a 456 g series airplane. Hey, there's a person who's trying to sleep! Grrr.

Why do flights allow a ridiculous amount of carry on luggage, but charge passengers for suitcases? People are bringing dogs, fifty-pound bags of uranium and all sorts of garbage on board the plane. Put it in your suitcase! You can afford a three-litre coffee, you can afford a decent case.

As soon as the pre board is announced, everyone immediately lines up like they are in the Soviet Union waiting for bread. The lineup is 50, 60 people long. Hello... It is assigned seating. You are not going to be given first class because you happened to be at the front. It doesn't work like that.

Check-In Attendant: Hey there, you are at the front of the line. You know what? This guy's a go-getter. First class!

Dummy: Wow, thanks! It pays to butt my way to the front of the line.

Me: Well, my ticket says 14F... so does that mean that I can sit in 14F?
Check-In Attendant: Wow. It sounds like we have a case of the "lazys". Apparently you thought taking a pee was more important than standing in line. There's a seat at the back... next to the washroom.

Quick follow-up to the story: we got on the airplane, and it was about a four-hour flight. There was a grand total of three kids on the flight, and of course, one was sitting right behind me. What is up with kids kicking seats? I get that the kid is eight years old. I understand that. Eight years have gone by—eight years of this kid annoying people on the planet. Well done, kid. And I get that he's excited, or he's a dummy, or he's got issues, or whatever. But why does that translate into legs flailing around uncontrollably? I get that the kid has no manners and is being disrespectful, but is he a kung-fu yellow belt or something? You don't see kids just randomly punching things, or having an uncontrollable desire to start chopping up carrots or something. Get me a Ginsu knife! I'm eight! It's always the kicking.
Another crazy question: they serve alcohol on the flight. Great. Sign me up. We as passengers have all these drugs, narcotics, prescriptions, uppers, downers and all sorts of mind-altering substances. Great. No worries. Are you telling me that NONE of these are allowed to be ingested by a small child? We have teams of scientists working around the clock, every day of the year, raising millions of dollars and fighting to cure AIDS, dementia, paralysis, and all sorts of awful diseases, and yet we can't come up with an aspirin or something that would knock a kid unconscious

for four hours? This is somehow beyond our capabilities of scientists?

My favourite part of the flight is when the flight crew announces that we are taking off. Put away the iPads, the iPhones, the electronic tablets, the tabletop hockey games, the Tetris game, the air hockey table, et cetera. Put it all away. Do you have a book? Put it down. Watch the safety demonstration. Pay attention! The greatest line of all-time:

"In the event of a sudden drop in pressure, the oxygen mask will deploy from the ceiling. Make sure to put it on yourself first before helping anyone else".

There aren't many guarantees in life, but here is one: you are telling people how to operate a seat belt, and unsuccessfully I might add, judging from the follow up that the flight attendant has to do when she wanders around and physically helps people put the one piece into the other piece. And then they are following it up five seconds later with how to operate an oxygen mask in the event of a nose dive into the ocean. This is NOT going to happen. I would actually love to see that: the airplane is struck by a meteor, the back half sheers off, and now people are getting sucked out of the aircraft. The guy who literally didn't know how to stick two pieces of a belt together using the clamp and the clicky thing is now going to suddenly navigate the dangling oxygen mask from the ceiling, deftly strapping it around his face before calmly helping those around him.

Mayor: Wow, thanks mister! You are a super hero! You are literally the greatest, most level-headed and calm person who has ever flown! Please take a ride in this limousine as we honour you in a ticket-tape parade."

The Guy: Sure thing. Hey, what's this mysterious belt-like apparatus sitting on the seat in the limo? I'm confused and scared.

The other total baloney part of the flight is that we can't use our iPad to waste some time during takeoff and landing. How much does an aircraft cost? A billion dollars? Five hundred million dollars? It's a lot of money, that is for sure. My iPad won't pick up wireless internet in the bathroom at the hotel because there's a metal stud in the wall, but somehow this powerhouse Apple product is going to take down an entire Airbus A380.

Can you imagine? We aren't allowed to bring on anything even remotely resembling a weapon: guns, knives, welding torches, or box cutters. (By the way, who's cutting all these boxes? How many boxes are you cutting that a knife is no longer doing the job? You now need a specialized tool called a box-cutter—this is all it does—cutting boxes up.) Anyway, according to the TSA, you can't bring box cutters (it's right at the top of the list – leave those shredded boxes at home, terrorists) gasoline, meat cleavers, scissors, golf clubs, pool cues, hockey sticks, ice axes or sabers. None of these are allowed. Yet, we are totally fine with bringing on board an iPad, which apparently has the power to totally disrupt the airplane. "We are preparing for takeoff. Please make sure to turn off all electronic devices." In fact, not using them is not good enough. Turning them off is not good enough. An iPad has an "airplane" mode which turns off everything in the iPad (wireless, Bluetooth, GPS, location services, et cetera). The flight attendants then walk around and really give people the gears when they see someone is powering down their device. "Turn that off, you criminal!" They will yell (albeit politely). How come the terrorists haven't figure this out yet?

Head Terrorist: OK guys, we need to really buckle down and figure out how to really inflict some terror here.

Lackey #1: I still say we should try to smuggle on board a bunch of pool cues.

Head Terrorist: I told you, it's never going to work. We don't even know how to play billiards.

Lackey #2: Ice Axes? Are they still banned?

Head Terrorist: I love the enthusiasm, but I am pretty sure that ice axes are still banned. Because the of the whole "axe" thing.

Lackey #3: What if one of us leaves an iPad turned on in their gym bag?

Head Terrorist: Finally! Someone is taking this whole thing seriously. Book your ticket and get going. Remember, don't embarrass us. Be careful and don't come back in one piece.

Movie People vs. Real People

I'm sure you have been in the following situation: you're watching a movie—it could be a big-budget action flick with tons of explosions and machine-gun bullets riddling the city. You know, summer entertainment. We typically love these kinds of movies. They are designed to take your mind off the every-day stresses of shuttling the kids to soccer practice. Nothing calms us down more than watching a dude in a metal suit shooting his repulsor rays at evil billionaires or aliens hell bent on taking over the world.

At some point during the cyborg-versus-freedom-fighter war movie, when the tomahawk missile is launched from the battleship that the aliens have commandeered, you are probably thinking, "wow, this is a little much. It's a little unrealistic."

Nope. Stop right there.

That's not the most unrealistic part.

It doesn't need to be a superhero movie, or a robots-turning-into-cars movie, or even a hunky-men-with-no-shirts shooting people movie. It can be any type of film, like a drama, or a television show. Basically it needs to have two people talking or doing stuff. That's about it. For me, the most unbelievable, outrageous thing in a movie is the way that people talk and behave.

Example: Hanging Up The Phone

In any drama on TV or in the movies, our main character is frantically talking on the phone, trying to get his police partner to meet up at the train station. The bad guys are there, and it is high time that they paid for killing the police chief at the start of the movie. This is it—the dramatic scene where our duo is going to get to confront the kidnappers.

"Let me tell you this," the hero says into the cellphone. "We need to get to Metro Station right now. If not... there will be hell to pay." Click. The hero hangs up the phone and starts running down the street. Wow what action!

No way. There is literally no way that this is how it goes in real life. Here is the way it would play out on real cell phones:

Hero: Let me tell you this—

Partner: Yes?

Hero: Yes. Let me tell you—

Partner: Yes go ahead.

Hero: I'm trying. Let me tell you this. Can you hear me now? [Long pause] We need to get to Metro Station right now.

Partner: Yes. I understand what is going on. I'm not an idiot.

Hero: I get that. If not... there will be hell to pay.

[Silence]

Hero: Okay, so I will meet you there.

Partner: Okay.

Hero: Alright.

Partner: Okay then.

Hero: I'll talk to you later.

Partner: Okay, bye.

Have you ever just "hung up" on anyone just as part of the normal course of a conversation? I'm not talking about "getting mad" and slamming down the phone, or telling someone off and then clicking the disconnect button. I mean, you are talking to your mom and you just end the call? "Okay, mom… Merry Christmas. That trip in the spring should be a good time." Click. Of course not. Even if it is the super villain calling and he is going to blow up the world... you still say goodbye.

Example: Not Telling Secrets

If you have ever worked in an office, or been to school, or ever been out of your house, or have any friends at all, then you will quickly see that this is among the most outrageous actions of any of the people in movies or television. In my fictitious show example, our protagonist has just saved the world by shimmying through an air duct, snapping the neck of the guard, and then blowing up the command central with a huge bomb. He avoids death by jumping out of the window (at the last minute—Academy Award for screenwriting, please) and grabbing a rope attached to the helicopter that is waiting for him. Nice work, hero! Fast forward to three minutes later, when the hero is being asked about what happened in the building.

Chief of Police: Johnson! You maniac! What happened in that building?

Hero: Let's just say... the situation got blown out of proportion.

[ROLL END CREDITS]

What? Are you kidding me? Here is the real-life conversation:

Chief of Police: Johnson! You maniac! What happened in that building?

Hero: OH. MY. GOD. You are never going to believe what just happened. Sit down. Sit DOWN. Okay. Now I am going to start at the beginning. Because this was just crazy!

And then for the next four hours, everyone that the hero has ever met will be listening to the same story over and over again.

Example: Getting Shot

I hate this one. There is no way that this would ever happen in real life. Here is the scenario: our hero has been shot in the shoulder. His partner wants to carry on to try to catch the bad guy. He's getting away!

Partner: Oh no! You've been shot!

Hero: It's nothing.

Partner: You're bleeding!

Hero: Forget it. Let's go catch The Skull.

Boo. Hiss. This is so ridiculous. Here is how it would play out in real life:

Partner: Oh no! You've been shot!

Hero: You got that right. Oh my god it hurts!

Partner: You're bleeding!

Hero: Well no kidding! I've been shot! In the body! What did you think was going to happen!

Partner: Okay, okay. I was just saying—

Hero: Duh, I was just saying. I was just saying. Call an ambulance, dummy! And forget about the bad guy. I am going into shock. I am literally going into shock. I'm having a panic attack right now. I can barely tweet this to my friends, I am so in shock. I'm sitting down right here on the curb until the ambulance shows up. And you are sitting with me. Argh, stupid bullet. This is so dumb! I'm just totally freaking out right now.

Example: Life Problems
I saved the most outrageous example for the end. This is crazier than all the blown-up trucks, missiles, aliens and cyborgs from the future—because this one features the person who wouldn't talk about themselves. Like the unicorn, they only exist in movies.
Our hero has just received some horrible news in the mail. They put down the letter and turn back to the birthday party in full swing. The wife knows that something is up.

Wife: Hey, Hank, this is quite the party! Hey… is everything OK?

Hank: Yeah. Yeah, honey... everything's fine.

Wife: Are you sure?

Hank: Yeah. Absolutely. [He folds up the paper and puts it in his pocket. Forcing a smile, he slowly walks out to the party.]

Terrible. Just terrible. This will literally never happen. Let's cue up real life:

Wife: Hey, Hank, this is quite the party! Hey… is everything OK?

Hank: NO!

Wife: Good Lord what is wrong?

Hank: I have CANCER!

Wife: Okay. Wow. That is awful. Can we talk about this after the party?

Hank: NO! In fact—hey, everybody, come in here for a second please! I have some terrible news about me and I would love to share it all of you! I can't wait to go to work on Monday and tell everyone there as well. Jerry, put down that coffee cake. I have some terrible news—about ME!

Road Rage

I don't know what is more stupid—people using the middle finger when they are driving, or the people who get truly, deeply, down-in-their-soul angry when they see it.

Here's the deal: most people are opportunistic, selfish bastards. I'm not telling you anything new. Have you ever driven past a fender-bender on the road? I'm not talking about the minor fender-bender where two distracted people are standing there, shaking hands and exchanging information. No... I'm talking about the four-car pileup with a body bag on the curb. And as you drive by, this is what you are thinking: Argh. I'm going to be late. Admit it! I know you by now. We've been through enough essays, and enough laughter and tears, that I know that you are a dick. But here's the key: so am I. We all are. We're all looking out for ourselves.

Which brings me to the middle finger. What is that? It's a finger. That's it. We are stuck in our cars. We're stuck behind the wheel, literally strapped in. We can't move. We can't get out, march over to your car, and punch you. Or, more likely, you get out and punch me. (I'm kind of wimpy.) The point is, we are like tied-down mental patients moving around at eighty or ninety kilometres per hour, and we don't like it.

As a society, we've tried to make driving more comfortable. We have all sorts of luxuries now built right into the car. It used to be that cars had cup holders. In the old days, cars also had cup holders: me. I would hold my dad's coffee when we made a trip in the old truck on Saturday to the landfill. I assumed that was why my parent's had me—basically to hold coffee and mow the lawn.

Cars nowadays have all sorts of luxuries. The heated seats? Great idea. The first time I ever turned on a heated seat, my body didn't like it. It was warm, I grant you that—but never having enjoyed a heated seat before, my brain was convinced that my body had peed itself. I hadn't done that for a long, long time. (Weeks, at least.) No, seriously, when you are five years old, you might pee your pants. It's warm, and then it's gross. Really gross.

Maybe some senior citizens pee their pants. It's not a big deal (hopefully), because they buy adult diapers. But really, between five and eighty? Those are the non-pee years. The whole reason we stop driving on long trips is to pee. If you are in the car... no peeing allowed.

I veered off topic. I am sorry. I was distracted. Which brings me to my biggest complaint: people are too distracted to even see me flipping them off. That is super annoying. If I go to the trouble of speeding up, passing another car and finally catching you, I would appreciate it if you would at least look at me as I jut my middle finger out and mouth obscenities at you from the adjacent car.

Everyone is looking at their phone in the car. I don't understand what is so important. I went for the first thirty years of my life without a phone. I didn't want the phone. Didn't need the phone. People try to phone me—I'm at home, watching television, and the phone rings. I don't even move. Sometimes I will glance over, which is mostly just a reaction. I have no intention of getting off the couch. Eventually, the phone message machine kicks in.

I wonder when we as a society are going to stop saying the "please leave a message after the beep" message. I'm pretty sure that even a third-world-nation citizen who has never had a phone before knows to wait for the beep. Who's talking immediately anyway? Wait for the beep—wait for me to stop talking first, and then wait for the beep.

I like when the message says "please leave your name and number." Well, no kidding. I want to know who is leaving the following message:

[Ring ring]

HELLO? HELLO? PLEASE PHONE ME BACK! IT'S AN EMERGENCY!

[Click]

I'm thinking that people actually do leave messages like that; otherwise, no one would be saying "please leave your name and number".

The worst is "hi, it's me." It's me? No, you are not me. I'm me. You're you. Which means you are not me. So I have no idea who you are. I once had a person phone me up and talk to me for five minutes before I finally burst their bubble and told them I didn't know who I was talking to. They were so crestfallen. Five minutes is a long time. It took me that long to realize that I was never going to figure out who this person on the other end of the line actually was. I was terrified that there would be an electrical storm, or I would have an aneurysm, or a meteorite would crash through the kitchen ceiling and I would never figure out who was on the other end of the line. I finally just blurted out, "you know what? I am so sorry, but I don't know who this is." In hindsight, I should have said, "you know what? I'm not sorry at all, by the way. But I have no idea who this is. And I don't care. Goodbye." Problem solved.

So my point is that I don't like phones. I still haven't figured out what is so important that people need to text or talk on the phone while driving. Maybe, just maybe if you were a surgeon and you were getting an emergency call. But even then: couldn't you afford hands-free? I mean, how bad of a surgeon are you that you can't afford a hands-free device for your car? You could probably even write it off as a business or a tax-deductible expense.

My other theory is that people are getting more and more easily bored. In the "olden days," people could watch movies and hockey games in top hats and dresses, and no one seemed bored. They would hold their monocles and carry around little handkerchiefs (I'm guessing to blow their nose?) and they wouldn't fidget. Gone With The Wind is listed at 238 minutes when you include the intermission. 238 minutes! Nowadays people have entire careers that are less than that. Times are different now. We can't even watch a half-hour TV show without the show itself trying to entice us to watch more. "Coming up after the break," it excitedly announces, "more trials of the rich and famous! Don't leave! Stay right there!" Too late—I have already changed the channel. After all, it has been forty seconds.

Lots of people like watching television and movies now while constantly playing on their phones, iPods, tablets, iPads, or whatever else they are inventing these days. Would you like to watch a movie? Yawn. How about watch a movie and flick birds with a slingshots at pigs? Now that sounds like an evening out!

So I'm starting to think that people are getting bored at the stoplights, and that's why they are whipping out their phones. Sometimes the light is red for thirty or forty seconds. We could be checking email or flicking birds on the small screen during that time. We need to have some sort of entertainment at the stoplight now. Maybe instead of a red light, we could have a little movie that plays. So don't be surprised if someday we are trapped at an intersection while a 30-second Twix commercial plays. We brought this on ourselves.

Getting Old

Turning twenty, thirty or forty isn't that big a deal, is it? It's always funny when someone turns a milestone age, like thirty—there's always someone in the peanut gallery who is super old, and they love to shout out, "I remember when I was forty! That's ten years older than you! I miss those days!" This isn't helping. Is this the fate that I have, laid out in front of me? I'm going to become the whiny, wistful old person? I guess that isn't so bad, since I am already a whiny middle-aged person.

Some old people like to exclaim, "you are only as old as you feel!" Have you ever noticed that it is only old people ever saying this? You never see an eight-year-old come in from playing with his action figures out in the front yard. "Sorry, mummy," the kid says, plunking down on the sofa. "I need a rum and Coke. I know that I'm only eight, but you are only as old as you feel, and right now I am feeling tired, cranky and sore. I'm like Grandpa—a seventy-year-old man who has a bad hip."

I recently turned forty. I don't feel any different than when I was sixteen, unless I start to think about it. Then I realize that I am definitely getting old.

The first sign is that any sort of sitting or standing involves audible groans now. Kids can be sitting in their bean bag chair and the mom calls out "ice cream in the kitchen!" and that kid bolts up like he's been Tasered in a bum cheek. Meanwhile, I get out of an $800 ergonomically-correct chair at the office and have to groan "hahhh...". Later on, I sit back down in the chair. "Hooo...". Okay everyone, I'm sitting down now. Here we go: one, two... hooo.

Kids never "sleep funny". You never hear about a kid waking up and eating his pancakes at the table while rubbing his neck. Adults, on the other hand, can phone in sick because they slept weird. "Sorry, boss, I slept on my right side instead of my left side. I can no longer feel my right side of my body or control my bladder. Yeah, yeah I know. I'm standing in my own pee right now. Crazy." When I was about seven years old, I accompanied by grandfather to work. I was on summer vacation and travelled out to British Columbia. My grandpa was a logger and he drove these massive trucks that hauled away the largest trees the forest. The wheels on these trucks are literally seven feet tall. These trucks are gigantic—and loud.

After four or five hours of sitting in this ridiculously loud truck, bumping our way along a windy, dirt road, I was sleepy. I was eight. It was the middle of the day and this truck sounded like a jet engine. It didn't matter. I was buckled into my seatbelt, but that didn't stop me—I just leaned forward and stuck my head between my legs. I was out.

I stayed that way for about an hour; my knuckles occasionally bumped along the floor of the truck cab while 130-decibel levels of tree-cutting carried on around me. My grandpa drove down the side of the mountain, the multi-ton load of fresh-cut trees weighing us down. I was completely unconscious. I guess he figured whether the kid was dead or sleeping, either way we had to get down the mountain and back home, so he might as well keep driving.

Fast-forward to today: if I drink too much water, I am up. There's no sleeping in. If there is wind outside, I am up. A floorboard creaks at 2:30 am, and I am up. You get into work the next morning, where everyone over thirty-five is walking around with bags under their eyes. "You couldn't sleep either? Argh, that wind! It was... blowing things around... no one can sleep." I don't remember going to school tired from wind blowing, but maybe I am selectively remembering things. I doubt it.

I caught myself visiting the other day. I was stunned. Friends of mine came over to my house and we chatted for about four hours. It was great! Remember when you were a kid? You begged, pleaded and whined your way out of the family visit. Why would you voluntarily sit in a living room with boring adults and talk? About stuff?

On a recent work road trip, I had about three hours to kill and I wound up listening to talk radio. It was the middle of the workday and I was bombing down the highway. Do you ever wonder who is talking on the radio at 10:00 am? These are phone-in shows, so the average slob gets a chance to talk on the radio. There's a reason that only professionals should be allowed on the radio. It turns out that people who are sitting at home during the weekday listening to the radio are angry at the government. If you are the president, or a senator or congressman, or even the mayor: don't turn on the radio during weekdays. There are a lot of angry old people phoning in to complain about everything from potholes to taxes. (Spoiler alert: they are against both.) Who listens to this stuff, I asked myself. Then it occurred to me: I do. I had been listening to it for about an hour. There were a couple of times where I silently wished I wasn't driving so I could phone in! Congratulations, and welcome to the Middle-Age Club.

Inconvenient Winter Olympics

I get that the rotation of the Earth plays a major role in a lot of what goes on—tides, the sun rising in the morning, blah blah blah. That's fine. But it is extremely annoying having the Winter Olympics over in Russia. I mean, the games are on during the workday. This is just another example of my career getting in the way of me sitting around watching TV all day.

I like watching hockey. The interesting thing is that during the Olympics, people who have never watched hockey, ever, are suddenly tuning in and screaming at the television. Okay, said the judge, I will allow it—you are patriotic. You can either sign up for the military, venture over to Kandahar and risk life and limb as a member of our proud Canadian Armed Forces, or you can wear an oversized Team Canada hockey jersey and high five me as I'm coming out of the bathroom at the Boston Pizza. Either way.

The women's Canadian hockey team played in the gold medal game against the U.S. in this most recent Olympics. The game was on at around noon my time zone (which is definitely not Russia) and so I was at my desk while the game was on. "No big deal," I quietly mumbled to myself. "I am PVRing the game just like I PVR the FA Cup soccer final, the World Cup soccer final, and the occasional Sunday Night Football game. No one cares and I will quietly slink home at the end of the work day and watch it." As long as I stay off Facebook, Twitter, Teaker, Tweaker, Reddit, Donnit, Seenit, and RedDogSeenIt Mobile App, I should be fine. Plus don't look at the elevator TV that shows all the news while I get down to the ground floor or listen to the radio on your way home from work. And don't look anyone in the eye—if they have a happy expression, that could be a hot tip on the final score.

Well, spoiler alert: everyone loves blabbing. The score was emailed out to everyone at my office. It was also on television in some office buildings, horns were honking by passing cars, and anyone wearing red was hoisted up onto strangers shoulders and paraded down the main streets in towns and cities all across Canada. So I figured out that Team Canada had won. Yes, I used the powers of deduction—I'm like the Sherlock Holmes of ice hockey.

Hey, no big deal! I will just go home and watch the game anyway. Except that the stupid PVR decided to be stupid and didn't record the game. it got the wrong channel, or something wasn't working right—I played back three hours of the People's Court and a cooking show. It just wasn't the same.

Hey, no big deal! I own an iPad and I figured I could watch the replay of the game, somewhere online. It's the internet, right? I Googled "Women's Olympic Hockey". No matter what you search for, Miley Cyrus comes up. Cancer. Miley Cyrus. Serbia in the 1990s. Miley Cyrus. Does she own the internet now? Only twenty minutes later I was able to locate CBC's replay of the game. I clicked on it. Here we go! Only that I had to download an app for the CBC Olympics.

Hey, no big deal! I downloaded the app. It only took another twenty minutes. (My internet might be a bit slow—an iPad has no moving parts but I swear I heard gears creaking.) I finally clicked "play" and got ready for the big game! First, however, there are five minutes of advertising. "The All-New GMC Whatever Truck."

Hey, no big deal! The first period started. I clicked through to the third period. Wow, what a game! I got all the way to overtime—it was tied! Then the app decided it didn't want to play "video" anymore. It was frozen on the goalie making a save. So I could hear the announcer screaming like someone was poking him in the groin with a pool cue, but I couldn't see anything—just the oil painting of the goalie.

I didn't want to just hear the goal—I was feeling like a diva and wanted to actually see it as well. I know... picky picky! I closed the app and relaunched it. It went back to the first period again. Oh well.

Hey, no big deal! I pressed "overtime" and suddenly I was watching overtime again. Yes! Only the app decided it needed to play 5 minutes of commercials again. So I am listening to the announcer yelling, and save after save is being made, and all the while I can hear "The All-New GMC Whatever Truck." Okay, okay, I get it—trucks are cool. Can I watch the game and listen to it at the same time? Is this allowed? Can I talk to the boss? Is

Miley Cyrus around?

I finally saw Team Canada score the big goal and it was a crazy, awesome game. So the app did work and hey I didn't pay a penny for it so I can't really complain.

Although I do have an overwhelming desire now to buy a GMC Truck.

The Mall

I recently had some extra overtime built up at work, and they made me take a day off in order to use it up. (I know, I know—a day off with pay—please don't feel sorry for me.) I decided to get an oil change for my car over at the car dealership. The good news: when I bought the car, they threw in four free oil changes! Cool stuff. The bad news: they are located across town. On the other hand, I guess you could argue that I am the slob who is located across town. Either way, it was a bit of a drive. Maybe it is a great opportunity to enjoy my new car? It sure felt like a chore driving across town, but then again, maybe it was awesome and I just didn't notice. (I'm not a car salesperson.)

So I travelled to this very specific automobile dealership to get my oil changed. It was 9:00 am on a Friday. Now, normally I work in an office during the day, during the week. I'm typical "office guy". I'm not out gallivanting around town during daylight hours like some socialite. This wasn't some quickie-get-change-fast oil change place, where you sit in your car while a bunch of mysterious strangers clink and clank underneath you while you are sitting in the driver's seat. (It feels like you are at the doctors and they are sticking a finger somewhere, but in car form.) No, this was much more high-end. I dropped off the car with trained professionals who would monkey with my vehicle completely out of site.

I decided that while my car was being operated on, I would pop over next door to the mall and "hang out" for an hour. Since I'm no longer a sixteen-year-old, "hanging out" for me means wandering aimlessly around the mall and shopping for books instead of bullying Steven, the weak kid in junior high school. Hi Steven! If you are reading this, I was not the one who kicked your binder down the hall—that was Richard. And, by the way, I agree, he is a doofus.

I want to make this plainly clear: it was not even ten in the morning yet. When the doors to the mall automatically swung open like I was boarding the bridge on Star Trek, I was flabbergasted to find that the mall was crawling with senior citizens. I mean crawling. There was one old guy lying on the floor who had lost his balance and I had to step right over him. No, I am kidding. We can tease because I didn't know who he was. Old people everywhere in the mall were laughing, shouting, and sipping their coffee. There was a lot of shouting. Turn up your hearing aids, people!

Every one of them had one small coffee and they didn't seem to be in any huge hurry to drink it. There must have been seventy or eighty old people, all hanging out at the mall. Having just turned "middle age" at forty, I am mentally predisposed to look at teenagers with a suspicious eye. If there were eighty teenagers all hanging out in the food court sipping coffee, or worse, doing drugs(!) I would have called the police. However, these were senior citizens. What is my appropriate level of outrage?

Curiously, I didn't feel any—if anything, I thought it was a little sad that they were spending a Friday morning at the mall sipping a small coffee. Man, this is your life? Sitting around? Drinking coffee? Laughing and talking with your friends? Instead of working? Hmm... actually the only depressing part of the whole thing was that there was one creepy guy over in the corner waiting for the Best Buy to open up, who was standing there trying to figure out how long before his car was ready.

Airplane Safety

I was sitting in the airport in sunny Mazatlan, Mexico. My vacation was over and it was time to go back to snowy, miserable Canada. The flight was going to board in about thirty minutes, which gave us schlubs about a half hour to wander around the duty free and investigate bottles of bourbon, play card games on the iPad and pretend not to secretly judge each other's tans before boarding the flight back home.

Suddenly the calm silence was interrupted by a voice on the intercom. A uniformed lady who either worked for the airline or had somehow broken in to the building and had gained control of the P.A. system announced that she had emergency exit seats available. Did anyone want an emergency exit seat?

For those who haven't flown much—these are the seats located in the emergency exit aisles, and they are highly coveted. They have more leg room and are quite the status symbol. It goes Pilot, First Class, Emergency Exit Row, and then finally the sweaty, tired masses. Then rats in the fuselage.

So we had emergency exit row seats available. Chaos erupted—people bolted upright in their uncomfortable 1950s-style kitchen seats and started bee lining for the check-in kiosk. It had suddenly turned into the floor of the New York Stock Exchange—hands were waving as if brokers were moving tons of pork bellies or dumping shares of an oil company hit by a typhoon.

I would like to announce that I was too good for all of this embarrassing tomfoolery. I would like to announce it, but it would not be true. I was in there like a dirty shirt. Something about my look—the wild, crazy eyes, the polite smiling that quickly turned into a motion of my finger across my throat, the ominous nodding... something worked. The airline lady gave me an emergency exit seat. I got my ticket changed and triumphantly returned to my little plastic seat to await boarding. Big wheel rolling through, people!

On the airplane, I sat like King Arthur at the round table. My legs were out, my arms were out—I was all stretched out, loving life. However, there is a dark side to this story—mainly the responsibility of being "the guy" in the emergency exit row. The flight attendant walked over and asked me if I understood the responsibilities of working the emergency exit window. Did I understand? Well, I figured in the event of a ten-thousand-foot drop in altitude, at least one of the bonehead passengers situated around me would have no problem "giving me their opinion" on what I should be doing. I nodded yes and found out that wasn't good enough.

"I need you to tell me that you understand," she said in a serious tone.

"Okay," I murmured, feeling sixty eyeballs on my hot neck. "I understand." However, here is my confession: I didn't understand. Well, not fully. I mean, I had a bunch of questions. Questions such as:

What happens if I try to open the door while the airplane is in flight? Can I do it? Will everyone get sucked out, including the guy behind me who is playing a slot-machine game on his iPad with the sound on full blast? Bleep, bleep, bleep! Pull the door— you're gone, and I'm the winner now.

Have the flight attendants ever been in an actual event like where the oxygen masks come flying out of the overhead area? They all seem so calm while they are putting on the masks during the demonstration. Can you do while you are screaming, crying and fending off the pervert in row six who figures this is the last forty seconds of his life, and he's moving in for a "quickie?"

If the airplane crashes and I am the only survivor, will that mean that I am the prime suspect? Is it like a "last man standing" thing, or an Agatha Christie movie, where the final guy is revealed to be the killer? Because I don't need to almost die and then have a bunch of people looking at me funny for the next thirty years. Not worth it.

If I work the emergency exit door, and everyone survives, will I finally be able to get a full can of Coca-Cola with ice, instead of the rinky-dink plastic cup? I actually think that even without an emergency, I should get the full can anyway—have you ever tried opening up that door with low blood sugar?

Something to consider: we all strap in, and then I open the door, and the one screaming baby goes flying out. Let's take a vote, and if two-thirds agree to it, I say we at least give it a try one time. It would be like a house of parliament. We all voted, I am sorry, it's not me, it is society, little Ricky has to go. Wah wah waaaaaaaaaah (I admit it is not really a question, but I do think about this a lot during air travel.)

I personally think that the safety instructions and the emergency exit duties are the biggest crock in the history of travel. No one is paying any attention to these rules. Do we honestly believe that if we are all flying along, having a quiet, wonderful time, and the wing snaps off, that everyone is going to calmly put on their oxygen masks, tighten their seat belts and then wait patiently for the plane to crash? And then—and only after me, the keeper of the emergency exit door—pops the hatch, that we are going to file out in an orderly fashion?

I guarantee you that if there was even a hint of a catastrophic failure, it is every man, woman and child for themselves. People would not only be putting on their oxygen masks, but they would be grabbing plastic forks in an effort to cut the hoses of their fellow passengers. "Sorry, but there's only so much oxygen..."

The airline staff would try to calm us down, but it wouldn't work. We get wound up when they run out of chicken during lunch, but we are going to be completely calm and rational as smoke billows out of the back third of the plane. Sure thing. You know that in the event of a real emergency, someone would immediately start yelling over the staff and try to get us to start claiming Jesus as our personal saviour. The ride is over people— you have thirty seconds and about twelve thousand feet to confirm your place in the afterlife! If we thought cell phone people were annoying and loud before, I can only imagine what the last two minutes on an airplane would sound like. "I love you! Can you hear me now? I love you? Hello? You'll never guess where I'm calling from! Hello? Turn down your stereo please..."

The greatest of all is after the actual crash landing—so at this point, we have survived the seventy seconds of plunging out of the sky and hurling towards the Earth, only to actually, somehow, miraculously land on the ground or in the water, and now—the emergency-exit guy is expected to pop the hatch and assist others to get off the airplane.

Are we aware of who wound up in the emergency exit row in the first place? Do we remember? The only reason I am sitting in the luxurious, extra-foot-space, cross-my-legs-and-laugh-at-my-fellow-passengers emergency exit row in the first place is because I pushed over a baby stroller and shoulder-bumped an elderly lady to get the seat back when we were about to board the airplane. These people are the ones who are now going to hang out and help out those people and their three hundred pounds of carry-on items off of the airplane as it sinks into the Atlantic?

I'll do it, but I want a full can of Coke. And extra ice.

ABOUT THE AUTHOR

Karl Wiebe was born in Toronto, Canada and currently lives and works in Calgary, Canada. Although he graduated university with a degree in business, his first love involves watching television and telling people to mind their own business. He currently works as a human resources trainer, developing courses, training materials and helping HR professionals.

Karl writes in addition to working a regular job. He is the author of his *Rants, Raves & Reviews* blog found online at www.karlwiebe.blogspot.ca.

He is the author of the novel *First And Life: My Year As A High School Football Player*.

For more writing, check out the website www.karlwiebe.com.

If you enjoyed this book, please consider posting a book review online or purchasing a copy (either printed or digital) for a friend. Or, if you didn't like the book very much, consider purchasing a copy for an enemy. Thank you for your support!

Made in the USA
Columbia, SC
29 November 2018